Tales From Southern Trails

Ryan Watkins

Copyright © 2017 by Ryan Watkins

All rights reserved. This book or any portion thereof may not be reproduced or used in any manner whatsoever without the express written permission of the author except for the use of brief quotations in a book review.

Printed in the United States of America

First Printing, 2017

Credits

Cover Illustrations: Michael Kittel
Copy Editor: Lisa Gatzen

ISBN-13: 978-1977706096
ISBN-10: 1977706096

Ryan Watkins
1512 Chattahoochee Circle
Roswell, GA 30075
www.mryanwatkins.com

Adventure Log

INTRODUCTION..i

JACKS RIVER &
BEECH BOTTOM..1

DAWSON FOREST WILDLIFE MANAGEMENT AREA.............23

TOCCOA RIVER &
BENTON MACKAYE TRAIL..37

WATERS CREEK TRAIL &
DOCKERY LAKE TRAIL..53

PANTHER CREEK FALLS TRAIL...67

COOSA BACKCOUNTRY TRAIL &
DUNCAN RIDGE TRAIL..81

BARTRAM TRAIL &
CHATTOOGA RIVER TRAIL..107

THE FOOTHILLS TRAIL &
KING CREEK FALLS TRAIL..143

Introduction

"TALES FROM SOUTHERN TRAILS" is a collection of stories from wilderness areas, parks and National Forests in and around the southeastern Appalachian Mountains. Most are in the state of Georgia, but there are a few stories featured in this work from South Carolina, Tennessee and North Carolina, as well.

This book is not intended to serve as a guidebook. Inside, you won't find elevation profiles, maps, technical trail descriptions or directions to natural landmarks from a remote National Forest parking lot. These stories are personal accounts of my experiences in places like the Chattahoochee National Forest, Cohutta Wilderness, Sumter National Forest, the Blue Ridge Mountains and other southern gems scattered throughout the region.

While I hope that sharing these experiences might help inspire your own outdoor journeys, there are many authors who have written far more nuanced descriptions of the locations you'll read about in this book. For more technical information on the physical characteristics of the trails included in this book, I recommend reading official and not-so-official guides, of which there are many available works to choose.

My goal from the beginning of this project was to document some of my favorite natural places near my home in the North Atlanta suburb of Roswell, Georgia. In this book, I attempt to blend my firsthand experiences with relevant historical and geological information on some of the places I've visited.

A few of the trip reports included in the coming pages, like my hikes along the Bartram Trail and through the Dawson Forest Wildlife Management Area, are sprinkled with tidbits on how past events and people helped shape the areas we're free to explore today. Other stories focus more on the trail conditions, my gear or the actual adventure itself. Sometimes, the forest or a mountain trail is merely a backdrop to a larger story. Every hike is different. As a result, each of these stories have a slightly different focus and tone than the others.

Regardless of where you live, you don't have to travel far to see something spectacular in the natural world. Many of these places have historical significance that can be uncovered through reading and exploration. Often, visiting these places firsthand is the best way to learn about them.

The one connecting thread through these stories is one of exploration. Sometimes these trips go as expected. Sometimes they do not. The nature of traveling, particularly venturing into the woods, means that we must expect the unexpected and be prepared for anything that may come our way. Injuries, wildlife, people, what we bring with us, weather and trail conditions are all variables that must be dealt with in the wilderness. It's how we handle these that make for compelling stories.

The southeast is filled with thousands of miles of diverse trails, rivers, scenic mountaintop views and majestic waterfalls. Almost all of these sites are accessible to anyone that wishes to go. You don't have to be an experienced backpacker to go to any of the places I've written about in this collection. In fact, you don't have to be an experienced outdoorsman to visit a vast majority of the Southeast's greatest natural spaces. The National Parks Service, as well as local and state park agencies, do an incredible job of ensuring access to many of these sites. Most are within a short walk from an easy-to-find parking lot.

Thanks to the plethora of natural landmarks throughout the region, the places I write about in this collection offer a variety of experiences. From mountaintops to river valleys and everything between, those of us who live in and around southern Appalachia are fortunate to be this close to so many outdoor opportunities.

The United States of America is not yet 250 years old (at the time of this writing, at least), but the history of the indigenous peoples goes back tens of thousands of years.

If you subscribe to the theory that the first humans to arrive in North America came across a land bridge connecting North America and Asia, supporting evidence suggests that these people first appeared on the continent more than 20,000 years ago.

A few thousand years after the first modern humans came to these lands, native tribes spread across much of North and South America, including the southeastern region of what is now the United States where the stories in this book are focused.

This area was once home to an immense population of native peoples from various tribes and communities.

Much of their collective story has been lost to war, disease and displacement, but the legacy of the indigenous people from this region continues to endure to this day.

These peoples, whose lands were stolen away bit by bit over many years, were pushed westward from their homes as settlers from Europe arrived to conquer the perceived wild lands of the North American continent.

The history of the early interactions between the native peoples of the Appalachian region and the settlers who came to eventually dominate the area is far more complex than I could ever understand or fully explore in a book like this.

The reality is that our past, and the many sins of our ancestors, have shaped our world into what it is today. Our National Parks and outdoor spaces offer more than an opportunity to connect with the natural world. These places can connect us to our heritage, as well.

But the connection from the past to the present when describing the region is as much genealogical as geological.

By most estimates, the Appalachian Mountains were first formed hundreds of millions of years ago and were once as grand as the Rockies or the Alps are today.

The world was vastly different all those millions of years ago.

These mountains existed long before what we consider modern man first walked the Earth and will continue to exist, in some form or another, for countless years to come, perhaps even outlasting humankind itself. Being in the woods, even briefly, ties us to the recent and distant natural past surrounding us all.

While trudging along a ridgeline, searching for spring water or struggling to summit a 4,300-foot tall Georgian knob with no switchbacks, it's easy to forget that you're walking along some of the oldest mountains in existence.

In this age of instant gratification and constant technological advances, it's all too easy to overlook cultural and natural history.

The Appalachian region is distinct and biologically diverse. And while not as physically daunting to explore as other parts of the world, Appalachia can offer a challenge to anyone with an explorer's heart.

Sometimes, it's not until a moment of quiet reflection after a day's hike that I find the time to truly appreciate my experience from a day on the trail. I've often, and I do mean often, struggled during a day's hike, but I've never regretted the experience, no matter how loudly I complained during.

The more difficult the challenge, the more rewarding the payoff, as the saying goes. This is almost always true for hiking and backpacking trips.

As our modern culture continues its headstrong push toward an inevitable all-digital future, I find the connection to my natural surroundings more important with each passing day.

The daily grind of life is a constant barrier between us and the world-at-large, but finding time to experience fresh air, living forests and nature's unexpected surprises is essential to my well-being. That's why I hike. That's why I encourage others to hike.

Explore nature, wherever that might take you. Take your friends and family along for the journey. Many of the trips told here were shared with my friends and daughter. It's my hope to inspire a love and appreciation of nature in her. But, there's plenty of her story in the coming pages.

I hope you enjoy these tales from southern trails and that you find the inspiration to tackle your own adventures.

Jacks River Trail & Beech Bottom Trail

I'D BEEN RESTLESS. A recent injury to my ACL kept me out of the wilderness for the last several months. I have missed the exploration and feeling of accomplishment that comes with an adventure in the woods.

My injury could not have come at a worse time. I hobbled through much of the fall on a swollen knee and didn't feel up for wandering the woods until the dead of winter, missing the prime hiking months of the year. The winter had been, so far, a mild one with cool evenings and warm, sunny days.

I made plans to spend a couple of vacation days to coincide with a friend traveling in from out of town. While he was off visiting family, I would head for the woods.

Testing my still-recovering knee was my major motivation. I also wanted to tinker with a few new pieces of gear that I purchased ahead of a planned multi-night backpacking trip a few months later.

I'd grown fond of the Cohutta Wilderness and the Chattahoochee National Forest over the last several years and often found myself there whenever time permitted. Cohutta is a typical Appalachian forest, dominated by hardwoods, varied elevations, rivers and miles of hiking trails.

The Cohutta Wilderness area, the second largest designated wilderness area in Georgia at more than 35,000 acres, was devastated by wildfires in the past year. During the peak of the blazes, more than half of the wilderness area was in danger of the blazes, but thanks to the efforts of many brave men and women (and a little help from Mother Nature), the fires were eventually contained before they spiraled out of control and charred the wilderness area into a blackened shell of its former self.

I recently discovered a section of the Cohutta that, at least at first glance, seemed promising for a long day hike. Jacks River, a 19.4 mile stretch of mountain-fed river, featured several trail networks of varying difficulty that had been spared from the fires. I planned a single-day, 18-mile section of trail that showcased several creek crossings and a waterfall regarded as one of the best in Georgia. Without the weight of a large, multi-night pack on my shoulders and challenge of climbing and descending numerous mountains, the distance would not be a problem if there was enough time in the day to walk that far.

My biggest concern was the weather. The afternoons had been warm much of the winter, but the mornings were still bitterly cold. The weekend of my planned hike was projected to be one of the coldest of the year.

I went to sleep the night before not knowing if I'd feel like hiking in the January cold when I woke the next morning. But as my alarm roused me, I was full of excitement and felt the longing to put a little dirt under my boots, even if the forecast predicted a mostly-sunny 32 degrees for the day's high.

I've never been bothered by hiking in the cold, especially if I'm prepared for the temperatures. Constant movement and warm layers can make walking in freezing temperatures feel no different than hiking when the temperature is in the mid-70s.

Whenever I've planned a trip like this, I wake up with my first alarm and jump out of bed to get ready without delay. Every other day of my life, I hit the snooze button way too many times before finally getting out of bed, driving to work and flopping into my desk chair at the last possible minute.

I wake with a smile whenever the mountains call. The forest, wildlife, mountains and views have always provided me with a contemplative happiness and feeling of contentment I continuously seek out in my everyday life but rarely find among the hustle and bustle of the modern world.

My heart is not at a desk in a cubicle helping a multinational corporation market insurance. My heart is in the backcountry wandering among the mossy oak and pine trees with dirt, rock and root under my boots.

I packed my gear the night before and needed only to shower and dress to head out the door. Once ready, I grabbed my dog and her pack, and hit the road shortly after the early morning sunrise.

Raven, a lab mix of some kind, was adopted a few months earlier from the North Atlanta Humane Society. She was a rambunctious dog, overly excitable and eager to run, jump and play at a moment's notice.

She was still a puppy, only around 20 pounds, and solid black save a small patch of white hair on her chin and chest that made her look older and more sophisticated than her eight months of existence, and puppy's temperament, might otherwise suggest.

Like most dogs, she was always willing to accompany me on a walk.

Raven, still anxious about riding in the car, quickly calmed down as we made our way onto the interstate heading north away from Atlanta in the early morning hours.

Two hours later, we arrived in the Chattahoochee National Forest. The paved roads gave way to gravel soon after crossing into the National Forest. Dirt, rocks and divots of mud dotted the old forest service roads. GPS has always been a godsend when attempting to find a remote trailhead like these. Long after a cell signal has been lost, the connection to the satellites floating thousands of miles above the earth somehow manage to keep us connected and en route to our destinations in the backcountry.

I followed through the forest along the gravel road for half an hour before we began to close in on our destination.

Large swaths of forest near the road had recently burned in the wildfires. Downed trees, charred logs and black soot covering the forest floor provided a sad and enduring reminder of the recent destruction as we slowly drove along. Despite the recent rains, the scorch marks were on full display. Some popular areas of the forest were still officially closed to campers and hikers.

Soon, we came upon Jacks River. A small, single-lane bridge crossed over the steady waters below. The narrow bridge was lined with tall, rusted side rails much the same reddish hue as the

Golden Gate Bridge in faraway San Francisco.

At the far side, the road forked into two opposite directions following the river both ways off to the left and right. The bridge seemed perfectly at home here.

The Jacks River trailhead was off to the right, while a river campground could be found a few hundred yards to the left. A handful of cars were parked in a lot near the campground, but I couldn't see any tent sites or campers from the road. I turned off to the right to find the trailhead.

A short distance from the bridge, the trailhead finally came into view. We drove on the old forest service road for quite some time, covering several miles before we arrived.

As we pulled into the parking lot for the Jacks River Trail, two weekend campers were finishing their final gear checks beside an old, rusted truck next to where we parked. Another beefy pickup truck sat next to theirs. After hopping out of the car, my dog Raven quickly ran over to the men, jumping on each excitedly, wagging her tail.

"I'm sorry!" I yelled as she took turns jumping back and forth between the pair. Raven sprinted off before I had the chance to clasp her into her harness.

"We just ate some bacon, I bet she smells that," one of the campers replied. I knew the real reason for the excitement was my dog's over-friendly predisposition and a complete lack of respect for personal space, but the smell of bacon probably didn't help her temperament.

We exchanged pleasantries as I grabbed Raven and secured her to the leash. Both men were older, probably somewhere in their late 50's or early 60s, and each carried a pervasive aura of a lifetime of outdoor experience. This was obviously not their first time in the woods.

Their packs were bulging, filled with all the requirements of a winter weekend in the forest. The gear and their packs were well-worn. One man, slightly larger in build than his partner, was wearing what appeared to be hunting apparel, complete with camouflage pants and a forest-themed jacket. The other wore jeans and a thick brown Carhartt jacket.

"Are y'all coming or going?" I asked before making my way toward the trailhead sign.

"We're comin'," the man in camo responded in a thick southern accent. "We got two buddies up the trail already, hopefully gettin' the fire goin'."

"Hey, if you see 'em," the other chimed in, "say somethin' mean to 'em, would you?"

Both chuckled and offered suggestions of things to say.

"Call 'em fat!"

"Tell 'em they're ugly," the other retorted.

"I'll make sure to tell them to make the fire good and hot," I said.

Both snorted at the incoming gag as we said our goodbyes. I could hear their continued laughter long after Raven and I made our way toward the trail.

The first stretch of trail followed closely alongside the river, which seemed fuller than I might have guessed given the drought the region experienced earlier in the year. There was no change in elevation to begin the hike.

The water was several feet deep and crystal clear, revealing a sandy rock bottom that would have made an excellent swimming spot in warmer months. As the chilly morning wind brushed against my face, I thought about how frigid the river must have been.

My inner-fisherman kept his eyes open for a good spot to cast a line in the icy waters. There were too many to count as the river began to change intensity, showcasing an impressive boulder field and white-capped flowing waters the further we walked upstream. Recent rainfall in the area helped swell the river after several months of neglect from one of the driest fall and winter seasons in memory.

The same rains that helped extinguish the recent wildfires in the area had also rejuvenated the river.

My father would have adored this place. His love of river fishing, and our camping adventures in my youth, left an indelible impression on me that I continue to carry to this day. This river, and its many good "holes," as we call them, were a sight to relish.

I stopped briefly by the waterside and looked for a sign of a rainbow trout.

Trout fishing was an outdoor tradition among the men in my family passed down through the last few generations. My grandfather, and the elder men of my family, spent countless hours in the North Georgia mountains during trout fishing season as an escape from their postwar lives and responsibilities.

This golden generation of my family experienced a smaller America, one not yet dominated by television, cell phones, overcrowding of outdoor spaces and all the trappings of modern life. Life was difficult for them, as well. But, there was a simplicity to the world then that some find alluring today.

Eventually, when my father was deemed old enough by the elders, he too joined the men on their river excursions. My father's own idea of the perfect afternoon in the wilderness is to wander alongside a mountain river, casting his line and aiming to catch the daily limit of rainbow trout. He has always seen the river, and fishing by extension, as his connection to the past and his family. New fishing gear, ultra-lightweight rods and unbreakable lines are nothing more than tools to help with that connection. What's always been important to him was just being there. Catching the fish never hurt, though.

The trail continued to gradually rise and fall beside the river, never climbing more than a few dozen feet above the water's edge. The river below was always within sight, and the sounds of the flowing water offered a soothing undertone to the wintry morning. The forest was calm and peaceful. The only sounds were our footsteps and those from the river a few feet away.

Cohutta had not yet awoken from its winter slumber.

Raven and I made our way along the river for a mile or so before we spotted the two campers mentioned to us earlier in the morning. The pair had already set up most of their campsite close to the water and a small campfire was burning midway between their tents, providing a smoky ambiance to the river valley as we approached.

Because of the wildfires over the summer and fall, a fire ban had been imposed in much of North Georgia for the last several months. Once the bans were lifted, campers returned to the North Georgia forests en masse.

Thanks to their earlier arrival, the pair seemed to have scoped the best two spots of the site. The campsite here was pristine, flat and free from obstructive trees near the water's edge. One tent was constructed just a few feet from the water's edge, while the other was positioned closer to the fire.

I stopped to talk for a few moments and deliver a promise made some 20 minutes earlier.

"Hello! Are you the guys with the two buddies back at the parking lot?" I asked as I approached the campsite. Both men turned and smiled.

"Oh, yeah. They still there?" asked the man tending the fire. "They're just waitin' on us to get the fire set up before they come down. Slackers!" Both men laughed.

"They are," I told him. "They asked me to tell you something mean, so, uh, you guys smell like ass."

The two men belted out laughter that echoed off the nearby rock wall and filled the surrounding area. This kind of practical joke must not have been new to this group. The campers were good sports and not at all surprised by the gag, almost as if they were unexpecting this kind of hijinks during their weekend stint.

After a brief introduction, our conversation quickly turned to my plans for the day.

"You aren't camping with that little pack, are you?" one of the men asked.

"Nah, I brought a lot of extra stuff just in case of an emergency. I'm just trying to see how many miles I can do today," I told him. "Worst case, I have a place to sleep tonight if I get stranded."

My daypack was the REI Traverse 28L National Parks Service Centennial pack. This pack was created to commemorate the 100th anniversary of the National Parks Service and judging by how many I've seen on the trail in the previous few months, it's become a popular choice for day hikers. Besides the functionality and reasonable price, a portion of the sale of each pack went to the NPS, a strong selling point for anyone looking for a capable daypack.

I've never had any complaints about the bag. It's light (two pounds, eight ounces), sturdy, and can handle more gear than is necessary for a traditional day hike.

Ultralight backpackers might be able to make do with the pack for camping if the trip was planned accordingly, though it's difficult for me to imagine someone being able to stuff the entire contents of an overnight trip inside the bag without making a few too many sacrifices to their own comfort.

For this trip, I packed a few extra supplies to fill the bag completely and to add a little bit of weight that might help acclimate my legs to carrying extra pounds again. Packs, even daypacks, function best when they are filled to near-capacity. For short jaunts in the forest, this often means carrying extra items and added weight to maximize the comfort from my pack. A half-empty, sagging pack can give a hiker just as many problems as an overfilled bag.

I stuffed a hammock, an extra jacket, summer sleeping bag, stove and pot, a dehydrated meal, fuel, water, snacks and a second pair of socks into the bag. I was not anticipating finding myself lost and alone in the Georgia wilderness overnight, but many experienced hikers have gone missing in better conditions. Even if I did find myself stranded, I hoped I could at least survive the night.

A few items were with me that never leave my bag: a compass, a knife, an emergency poncho, a toiletry kit, trowel, flashlight and my pack's rain cover. These items are necessary whenever you venture into the backcountry alone, even for just the day. While I've never experienced a moment of panic on the trail due to losing my bearings or an unexpected turnaround, the day may come where I find myself lost and in need of more than a bottle of water and pack of peanuts to keep me alive.

Having these items in my bag has always helped mitigate the anxiety that accompanies the fear of the unknown.

Raven carried a Lifeunion Saddle Bag Backpack specifically made for dogs I purchased online a few weeks earlier. This was the first trip for her with the pack, but she had a few days' experience walking around with it on in my apartment and seemed unfazed by the straps and extra weight on her back. After a few short hikes with the bag, she grew accustomed to wearing the harness and understood that putting the pack on meant going outside. I was surprised how well she took to it right from the beginning.

I packed two cups of dog food, several doggie waste bags and two small collapsible bowls inside her bag. Unfortunately, Raven's pack was too small to fit any water, but hiking beside a river and its many runoff tributaries offered plenty of water sources for her. I hoped to slowly acclimate Raven to carrying more weight, as well.

I was envious of the campsite now in front of me. Even if it was predicted to drop well below freezing during the overnight hours, the forecast showed only a small chance of overnight rain. A steady campfire, warm layers, a hearty sleeping bag and hot food could go a long way this weekend.

Part of me wanted to set up my hammock and impose myself on the experience, but Raven and I had our own adventure to experience. Besides, I questioned whether there was enough gear in my pack for a comfortable overnight trek in summer, much less a bone-chilling winter's night. It would have taken quite a bit of extra planning and much more gear to make an overnight possible in these temperatures.

After chatting a bit about the trail and the river, Raven and I said our goodbyes and continued toward Jacks River Falls. The trail followed alongside the river for another mile or so. The path below our feet was soft sand and stone with the occasional large rock jutting upward through the ground but nothing tricky. Jacks River here featured massive boulders that were situated directly in the water, which cut around the boulders, slicing the river in two.

The path narrowed and the water's edge moved closer to our right. Eventually, we were walking along rocks themselves, and I began to wonder when the trail would open back up into the pleasant rock and sand path we were walking on only a few moments earlier.

Suddenly, the trail stopped directly in front of us without warning. Looking behind me, I could no longer see an actual trail. To my left was a rock face and to my right was the river. Ahead of me was impassable brush and what I assumed was more rock face above the river.

We were at an impasse.

I turned to see if we missed a turn somewhere along the path, but there was nowhere to go but back in the direction where we had come. "Maybe we have to cross the river," I wondered aloud, hoping I was wrong.

Then I saw it, a rectangular blue blaze on a tree far across the river along the opposite bank confirming a crossing.

"Oh, shit. Well, that sucks."

Before attempting the hike, I read about creek crossings on the

Jacks River Trail, but this was no creek. I assumed that the worst of these crossings might involve slipping from a flat rock into ankle deep water or wetting the bottom of my boots. This river was several feet deep at the very minimum.

I scanned for a place to cross without having to wade through the water. Maybe there were rocks to hop along? Maybe there was a bridge I missed? But, it was useless. The only way across was to take off your boots, hike up your pants and march through.

I shivered at the mere idea of crossing the river in these temperatures. "I'm not prepared for this," I told Raven while contemplating what to do next.

The water was briskly moving downstream, and the river seemed as though it would come up to my waist or higher if I hopped in. Crossing here in tennis shoes and shorts during the summer was probably a wonderful experience. Crossing in the winter without waders or tall boots was out of the question.

Like I told Raven, I was not prepared.

Disappointed, we turned back. I stopped at a riverside campsite and took off my pack for a while. I sipped water, snacked on peanuts and thought of what to do. I seriously considered hanging my hammock, putting the sleeping bag underneath me and taking a nap before heading back home before the mid-afternoon sun fell behind the hills, but that was not an option.

We had only been in the forest for a few hours by that point in the day, and heading home this early would be a waste.

After a while, I resigned to hiking back to the car to find another trail leading to the falls.

Heading back, we soon returned to the now full party of four at the riverside campsite. The two campers we met in the parking lot earlier in the morning were now setting up their tents while the other two sat by the well-deserved fire. Smoke bellowed.

"Did you make it up to the crossing?" one of the men by the fire asked.

"I did," I told him. "I didn't realize it would be that kind of creek crossing. I'm totally not prepared for that."

He was not surprised.

"There's a spot where you can hug the rock wall and go up a lil' bit further. We come up here every year and have looked a bunch," another chimed in. "We've never really been able to find a way up, though."

We talked for a few more moments before saying our goodbyes. Raven and I continued to the car, arriving back to the trailhead a short while later.

After reviewing the information board in the mostly empty parking lot, it was time to find another way to the falls. According to the map posted, there was another way, but it required a lengthy drive up an old mountain road. We piled into the car and headed off for Beech Bottom.

I love driving my SUV up and down forest service roads.

Navigating the bumps, the loose rock and sudden drops off the ridges make for exciting driving. You simply can't find untamed and wild roads like that in the city. At least not my city. Pot holes? Sure. Those are everywhere. But pot holes are no fun.

The drive to the second trailhead was gorgeous. The climb from the valley below seemed to go on forever, higher and higher. After several miles, winding left and right, further and further up, we came to the parking lot for the Beech Bottom trailhead. At this point, I was convinced we had driven all the way to Tennessee. After getting home and checking a map of our adventure, I realized we did indeed make it to the Volunteer State that afternoon.

At our highest point, my phone buzzed with the familiar notification of missed calls, text messages and social media alerts. As we approached Beech Bottom, cell service was again lost.

As expected, there were no cars at the trailhead, but there was a single Bud Light can sitting in the middle of the makeshift gravel lot. It doesn't matter where I go in Appalachia, there's always a Bud Light can sitting somewhere near the entrance of a trail.

Why is it always a Bud Light can?

The winter afternoon peaked by the time we arrived at our second destination of the day, and the sun was beginning its slow crawl toward the horizon as we climbed out of the car. I guessed there were only four hours or so of daylight before the sun fell completely behind the neighboring mountains and tree line, making any hiking after the next four hours a potential night hike.

After eating a quick junk food lunch, I grabbed my pack, harnessed Raven and took off toward Jacks River from Beech Bottom knowing we were fighting time.

The trail began with a slight decline in elevation but featured a bit of up and down as we progressed along. We met with a handful of small creek crossings on the way, but nothing deeper than an ankle. These were actual creek crossings, able to be hopped over or walked through without soaking through my boots, not at all like those fake crossings across the Jacks River that were as deep as a swimming pool.

Raven charged through the water after a bit of initial hesitation on the first crossing. I was surprised by the routes she took as she mowed ahead of me throughout the day, staying out of the mud and trotting along on the softer bits of the trail like the oft mossy, elevated banks where few hikers step.

Raven would often get as far ahead as comfortable with the leash, pause to turn around and see if I was still behind her. She repeated this gesture throughout the day. It was comforting to know that she was concerned about whether I was still with her. Maybe she found comfort in knowing I was behind her, too.

From what I previously read, the Beech Bottom Trail was a shorter, quicker and less strenuous path to Jacks River Falls than the Jacks River Trail we hiked earlier in the day. This appeared to be true as we walked on, stopping periodically for quick breaks and sips of water.

As we made our way along a relatively flat section of trail after coming down from the ridgeline above, I heard a rustling and commotion up the trail that sounded eerily like sounds made by black bears I encountered in the Smokies a year earlier.

I stopped and whispered to Raven, "Oh shit, I think that's a bear."

We peered around a bend in the path, only to see a massive black creature digging and foraging alongside the trail about 20 yards ahead of us. This creature was massive. Somehow sensing our presence, it picked up its head, snorted and looked around. I immediately recognized it as a wild mountain boar. Raven let out a growl and began barking as violently as any 8-month old puppy could muster at the sight of the wild beast.

My heart raced as I fumbled for my hip-pocket camera, but it was no use. The boar sprinted away from us at breakneck pace up the trail, sticking to the path for as far as I could see. Raven successfully chased the boar away before I could even unzip my camera's pouch.

"Get him," I encouraged Raven as the giant animal faded off into the distance down the opposite direction of the trail. This was my first-ever encounter with a wild boar. Not only had I never approached one, I had never actually seen one in the wild before.

"Why did I go for my camera instead of my knife?"

As if a pocket knife would have done any good against a 300-pound wild animal that moved as swiftly as a nimble greyhound. Still, I thought it interesting that in the heat of the moment, photographing the creature was more of a priority, at least in my subconscious mind, than running away or fighting it.

I paused for a few moments before continuing down the path to allow the boar plenty of time to escape off into the woods, occasionally yelling out "Hey boar! Hey boar!" as I slowly made my way forward with a pounding chest.

The encounter spooked me. I wondered what would have happened if it tumbled toward me instead of running off in the opposite direction. What would I have done? I probably would have fumbled for my camera until I was trampled to death.

The run-in only encouraged Raven's instinctual guard dog mentality. She sniffed and eagerly pulled ahead, anticipating another wild pig or something even grander just around the next bend. Knowing that she was on the prowl, her pack mentality helped settle me as we continued down the trail back to the river. Hopefully, the pig told all his friends that we were making our way through the woods, and they would all stay away.

After another mile or so of cautious hiking, we made it to the bottom of the valley, back alongside the Jacks River about seven miles upriver from where we attempted to hike earlier in the day. If we continued under ideal circumstances from our original starting part that morning we might have been at the same place by this point in the afternoon.

This trail intersection by the river here was confusing. There were only fifteen minutes or so left in the day before I planned to turnaround to head back to the car and off the mountain to avoid hiking in the dark. The trail forked with one path heading to the left and the other off to the right. Neither direction clearly indicated the way to the falls and trail signs were scattered along both paths.

There were several signs warning against camping alongside the river, scattered among what must have been, at one time, a stellar campground. There was also a large sign restricting the use of horses past a certain point along the path. We made our way off toward the area with the horse restriction, thinking that is where we'd find Jacks River Falls.

I was happy to have hiked the four miles down the mountain to the river in the two hours I gave myself, but the hike out would be a steady uphill that would cut into my available time.

The success of my out and back depended on how quickly I could make it back to the car while racing against the setting sun. We didn't have much time to explore the river.

"I should have just come here first," I told Raven, seriously regretting starting at the Jacks River trailhead earlier in the day. An entire day here would have meant a mostly leisurely hike, plenty of time to relax by the water's edge and an opportunity to explore the area in complete solitude.

I dropped my pack against a tree and jogged off toward the direction I thought the falls might be, Raven wagging her tail as she followed closely behind.

It was no luck. I went as far as I could alongside the banned and abandoned campsites stopping to listen for the falls every few minutes. The river was wild, but there were no immediate signs of the falls anywhere around us.

Eventually, our time ran out. We were forced to head back toward the junction without finding the waterfall. After gathering the pack once again, we started the slow march up the hill toward the trailhead, disappointed in missing out on the sight after an already long day of hiking.

The walk back was far less eventful than the hike down. We already experienced the creek crossings, the views and the chance encounter with a boar. There were no other hikers on the trail that afternoon and the only people we had seen since arriving in the forest were the hearty old campers from earlier in the morning. The incline made for a slower hike, as well, but our surroundings continued to impress.

About halfway back up the hill, we stopped for a short snack and water break near a group of recently felled trees on a ridgeline clearing.

Raven was exhausted by this point in the day, panting and lying down whenever the opportunity presented itself. My legs ached from the pace of the climb away from the river and the valley now hundreds of feet below us.

I snacked on some peanuts and drank as much water as possible while Raven lapped up a bowl of water, as well.

"Good dog," I told her. I wondered what she thought of the boar from earlier in the day.

After our snack break, we continued back toward the car. The sky began to darken as the sun continued its long fall behind the tree line above us. An hour or so later, we arrived back at the car, just over four hours from when we started the Beech Bottom Trail earlier in the day.

The hike from the river to the parking lot featured a gentle incline but an incline nonetheless. And while there were a few minor obstacles, like creek crossings or a few fallen trees covering the trail, the walk was enjoyable nonetheless.

We were tired but only physically. After crawling into the car and securing Raven in the front passenger's seat, I sat for a moment to catch my breath and reflect on the day's journey.

Jacks River and Beech Bottom had not gone exactly as planned. The unexpected river crossings, the morning cold and not finding the waterfall were major disappointments, but the forest offered a few firsts that day. This was Raven's first full day's hike, and I experienced my first encounter of a wild boar. That was a memory I hoped to carry with me for a long time, even if only as a cautionary tale.

The forest had been quiet and peaceful. The day of near-solitude offered a chance to forget about the recent stress of life and to connect, even briefly, with the natural world once again. Despite the sore feet and tired legs, my spirit was rejuvenated.

The day may have brought a few challenges, but it came with its own unexpected rewards.

Dawson Forest Wildlife Management Area

TUCKED AWAY IN REMOTE Dawson County, Georgia is a mysterious, sprawling woodland known as the Dawson Forest Wildlife Management Area. Sometimes called "Georgia's Area 51," the WMA was once home to an experimental aviation and nuclear testing facility owned by aerospace firm Lockheed Martin but now exists as an outdoor recreation area with dozens of miles of hiking trails and many other natural attractions.

Long after the facility's decommissioning, rumors persisted about the purpose of the old concrete bunkers and abandoned topside buildings of the Georgia Nuclear Aircraft Laboratory (GNAL). Because of the governmental secrecy surrounding the site during its heyday in the 1960s, local residents, especially those with long memories, have a host of stories and conspiracy theories ranging from alien abductions and UFOs to mutated deer and malformed plant life about the area.

The internet is rife with accounts of unnatural occurrences at the WMA. Mysticism and conspiracy aside, there is an indescribable quality about the WMA that adds to the overall experience in ways most outdoor recreation areas simply cannot match.

It's creepy.

The laboratory was shut down and sold to the City of Atlanta in the early 1970s after the dream of nuclear-powered aircraft fell out of favor with the science, military and aviation communities.

City officials originally intended to use the land to build a second airport to deal with the Atlanta population boom, but the area was later deemed unsuitable for a variety of reasons. Atlanta, which to this day still owns some 10,000 acres of the forest, eventually ceded control to the Georgia Forestry Commission, and the outdoor recreation area was born a few years later.

I was unfamiliar with the history of Dawson Forest while looking for a suitable afternoon hike one fall Saturday. While scanning my usual websites and online forums for suggestions and trail maps, I came across a series of trails in the WMA that I thought would make an enjoyable day's trek.

Joining me would be my daughter Lucy and friend Mike. Mike hiked with us before, most notably along the river trail at Panther Creek a few months earlier. His experiences in the Canadian Rockies as a child instilled in him a love for nature and the wilderness exploration that I hoped to pass on to my daughter.

Lucy, even at age six, was a seasoned pro by this point in our weekend adventuring. We'd hiked together dozens of times and put almost 100 miles under our boots together in the last year alone. I considered myself fortunate to spend so much time with her in the car on the way to and from the trails and on the actual trails themselves. I hope that she looks back on these trips fondly when she's older, in much the same way that I look back on trout fishing trips with my father.

Our conversations on the trail often revolved around life, school, cartoons, jokes, stories from the past, social issues or whatever else might come up. We've played games, like "21 Questions" or "I Spy" while plodding along to help stave off any potential boredom. Keeping Lucy entertained, at least mentally, also helped keep me focused on her experience.

Like most six-year-olds, Lucy is excitable and easily distracted if not constantly stimulated. Hiking the trail can sometimes be physically difficult for her, which is why I've always tried to include some sort of payoff on our hikes like a mountaintop view, a lunch snack on a river's edge or a waterfall to stand atop. We've always taken our time to finish a trail, and I've always set aside enough time to finish a trip with plenty of time to spare.

For this trip, the planned payoffs were four waterfalls scattered throughout the forest and several rivers to see along the way. The elevation profiles I read beforehand indicated a relatively easy and mostly flat trail network throughout the forest.

Lucy and I awoke that morning and packed our hiking bags. We shopped the night before for trail snacks, water and other provisions that we loaded into our packs in the morning.

Lucy carried her REI Sprig 12 youth backpack (in pink, of course). Inside, she carried water, a small plastic grocery bag for trash, an extra pair of socks and snacks for the day, including her favorite trail meal, a Lunchables.

She also brought with her a small wooden hiking stick, complete with inlaid turquoise stones and horsehair that we purchased a few months earlier from a North Georgia flea market during another weekend mountain adventure.

Lucy adored her hiking pole, and it was one of her first pieces of gear she carried that was specifically for her. For many of her early trips, Lucy would hike with only the pole while I carried all the water, snacks and other necessary gear. The pole became an extension of her body while on the trail. She would never tackle a trail without it.

I filled my daypack with my hammock and straps, a lunch, my summer sleeping bag, a tarp, my cook kit, a change of clothes, my knife, trowel, compass, toiletry sack, a flashlight and a few other small items that I used to weigh me down and fill up the pack.

I often carry more gear and weight than is necessary in hopes that I'll be somewhat acclimated to a full 65-liter pack when the time comes. My day pack, with food and water, is rarely over 10 pounds, even with all the extra gear and water included. Lucy's pack weighed around a pound or two.

Lucy recently began carrying her own food, water and whatever else she could fit into her pack that she deemed necessary to the experience. The weight of her food and water was not an issue for me, but in an effort to immerse her into the experience, I wanted her to take a bigger role in the hike and introduce her to the idea of supporting herself. For me, this meant gradually working up to Lucy carrying her own supplies.

Mike had arrived at the apartment a little before nine that morning after we had packed all our gear. He brought along his hiking pole and a backpack filled with his lunch, a few snacks and some water. After a bit of catching up and a discussion of the plans for the day, we made our way to the car to head to the WMA.

Our trio arrived at the entrance to the Dawson Forest an hour or so after leaving my North Atlanta apartment. An unmistakable sense of a manufactured experience oozed through the forest. Old paved roads and the flat remains of concrete pads where large buildings once stood stuck out like a sore thumb against the natural, tree-lined backdrop.

There were chain-linked fences all along the parking lot impeding the sense of wild wonderment I often feel immediately before embarking on a hike. No Trespassing signs were carefully placed along the fences surrounding us, warning against investigating the building remains too closely.

These woods were different, but we didn't yet know why.

"There used to be something massive here," I told Mike as we parked. Initially, I thought the area might have been home to a fairground or some other seasonal or temporary structures. Maybe this was an old farmer's market or food storage depot?

There were a few small campsites set up in and around the parking lot. Most of the vehicles parked there were trucks with massive horse trailers in tow. I did not realize prior to the hike, but the Dawson Forest was one of the premiere horse trail networks in North Georgia, and it appeared every horse in North Georgia was here on this day, as well. Judging by how many horse trailers were in the parking lot, there must have been a dozen or more horses in several groups making their way through the forest as we prepared to set off.

We quickly scanned the information board and picked up a paper copy of a map of the area, detailing the trail networks and some of the nearby attractions. We decided to attempt a loop, roughly nine or ten miles in length utilizing the WMA's red and blue trails. There were trail access fees for horse riders and mountain bikers posted on the board, but both parking and hiking the trails came without cost. Lucky us.

Disembarking the trailhead for the woods meant walking next to a massive, multi-story and long abandoned concrete building fenced off from the rest of the area. Overgrowth encroached to the fence by the trail, blocking much of the view beyond, but the old structure peaked high enough that the top half of the building was still clearly visible to all passersby. Dozens of signs that warned against trespassing were plastered all along the fence, here more than other areas of the WMA we had seen so far.

Our group quickly moved beyond the abandoned concrete structure and made our way through the forest through a short, green tunnel of foliage. This opened into a larger section of trail, possibly an old forest road that continued down a short hill toward a sprawling area.

The first major stop was a wooden overlook built beside a quickly drying swampy pond a few hundred yards down the trail. The three of us walked down the bridge to the covered overlook and went inside the man-made structure. A small window cut into the side of the building looked out across the pond. The depth appeared shallow, and dried mud-cracked islands dotted the water, suggesting a much fuller pond at some point in recent memory.

Our summer drought had extended well into the fall, and ponds with trickling water sources, like this one, were suffering as badly as local reservoirs like Lake Lanier.

Out on the water sat a single crane with its sharp eyes on the water below, ever-ready for its next meal. Once or twice, we saw large ripples press out against the water from below the surface, a suspicious sign of a lively fish, perhaps on a hunt of its own. Lucy was enthralled with the bird, who seemed to own the pond and all of its underwater inhabitants. Eventually, though, it was time to move on, and we made our way back to the trail.

Shortly after the overlook, we experienced our first section with horse droppings. Massive piles were scattered along the trail every 10 feet or so as we made our way into the wooded area and away from the pond. Some of the droppings were fresh, while others had been left behind for a while. Dodging the piles became a sort of game for us. It was impossible, however, to dodge the smell. The trail reeked with an unpleasant stench that we simply could not escape no matter how far we walked.

Continuing up the trail and deeper into the woods, the unmistakable sound of a shooting range slowly became louder and louder. Eventually, the sound of pinging bullets against metal targets turned into a real distraction.

The early sections of trail left much to be desired between the constant pinging and blasting of faraway firearms and dodging the horse droppings left on the trail that required constant attention to our feet. Trash was scattered in every possible nook and cranny. Beer cans, empty water bottles and other various bits of trash were seemingly everywhere.

We had barely begun the hike, and I was already disappointed in the conditions. At first glance, it seemed the WMA did not seem to receive the same kind of care that other, more popular spots, were accustomed to receiving. Perhaps the visitors here did not have the same respect for the land commonly found in more remote areas of the wilderness.

I've always stressed to Lucy the importance of keeping an eye on your feet, but this was even truer today. Whether it's a large rock or mud, there's always something to avoid on the trail below. Lucy kept her wits about her and avoided the large horse patties littering the trail with only a few occasional reminders.

We kept moving until we came to a little clearing in the woods where we encountered our first group of horseback riders. We stopped to rest, drink a bit of water and chat with the riders.

Lucy was in complete awe. What little girl doesn't dream of owning her very own horse? She was able to pet a few of the massive creatures, which only stoked the flames of envy in her eyes. It was tough explaining later why she couldn't have a horse in our two bedroom North Atlanta apartment.

"I guess you have to get her one now," one of the women in the group shouted to me as they rode off up the trail.

Gee, thanks, lady. I'll get right on that.

A few moments after the horses trotted off down the hill, a father and his son, around Lucy's age, came toward us from the direction we were headed next. They were out for a day hike but turned around for the day well before noon. We exchanged pleasantries and discussed our day's plans before quickly moving on.

Determined to get as many miles as possible into the day before the afternoon wore on, we pushed on toward the Etowah River, one of the two main rivers that flow through the WMA area. Even if the trail itself was a complete disaster, I still wanted to see as much of it as possible. The elevations here were not strenuous. While the trails were not entirely flat, the gains and losses were minimal at best. This made for easy mileage early in the day.

Our small group crossed over a creek bridge and ultimately made it to the Etowah, walking beside the flowing water for a short while before the trail diverted back into the woods. At a junction, a small path led back to the river again while another drove further into the forest. We walked to the end only to find a massive concrete bunker, perhaps some sort of drainage system for a larger complex below, buried into the rock leading into the river.

We wondered what once existed here and what might now, all these years later, be under our feet.

A mile or so later, we came across a large black rat snake moseying through the leaves along the side of the trail. I was ahead of Mike and Lucy and quickly paused when I heard the familiar rustling of a creature through the fallen, dried leaves. I stopped and glanced down, seeing what first appeared to be black rubber or plastic piping. But almost as quickly as it was spotted, the tube slithered ahead a few inches through the golden-brown leaves. After a closer look, I realized this was indeed no plastic piping.

I pulled Lucy close to keep her calm as we looked at the creature sitting a few feet off the trail for a moment or two before pressing on. Lucy has experience with animals on the trail, but as unpredictable as wildlife can be, I've often preached vigilant caution. The snake, possibly a black racer, was docile and still.

His small head popped up behind a fallen orange leaf to check us out as we began to move forward again, but we were far more interested in him than he was in us. We pressed on toward the river, leaving the little creature alone in peace by the side of the trail.

Eventually, we came to a junction and switched trails as we made our way back toward the river. The worn path here was more remote, and as we moved further into the forest the sound of gunfire slowly faded away behind the small hills and plethora of trees. The trail narrowed here, as well, and became less friendly for horseback riders. Soon, there were no signs of recent riders anywhere along the path. We had finally hiked further into the forest than the horses who so graciously left the patties.

Thanks to the never-ending tangles of spider webs across the trail itself, I could tell we were the first people to walk this trail that day, perhaps even longer. I gave up picking the strands out of my beard and resorted to swinging my hiking pole up and down in front of me as I walked. This was effective. I imagined Mike and Lucy appreciated my efforts as they followed close behind.

With the faded gunfire and spider webs under control, my impressions of the trail lifted. After some two hours into the day, it finally started to feel like a proper walk in the woods. The less populated and utilized area of the WMA felt more natural and trash here was few and far between.

The trail ended abruptly at the Etowah. Across the other side of the bank was the continuation of the path that required hikers to wade across the small river to reach the other side. We debated for a few moments on whether to continue through the crossing. Mike seemed keener to go across than I did, perhaps because he would be able to cross without having to carry a child and all her hiking gear, as well.

We decided to walk up the hill next to the trail to rest and have lunch while we discussed what to do next. Mike had brought a massive grocery store deli sandwich, while Lucy and I ate Lunchables.

As we snacked, a handful of kayaks flowed down the stream below us. Each of the kayakers carried a bit of fishing equipment with them, but it seemed to me to be too late in the day to effectively fish for trout in the river. Maybe they were heading to set up camp to fish at dusk or back to their cars to return home.

There were several beer cans at our resting spot, quite a bit of cardboard trash bits, several plastic grocery bags and even an empty gallon jug sitting next to a small fire ring where we sat for lunch. We piled the trash as best we could into a makeshift fire ring, hoping someone with a proper trash bag would eventually come along to clean up the mess.

Before we left our lunch spot, a solo rider on horseback rode into the river from the bank beside us, dropped a sponge into the cool water only to lift it up and wet his horse's neck. He repeated this several times before riding off across the water and up the opposite bank. This was a sight to see. Lucy, again, was in awe and completely forgot about her lunch for a moment or two.

After finishing our lunches and packing away what trash we could carry, we turned back and walked back toward the road, this time turning left to follow the river back to the red trail we were on earlier in the day. Much of this walk was on the hard gravel road. A lone trail runner came toward us and passed by without a fuss, though he did seem to pick up his pace once he noticed us heading toward him.

Several cars were parked at a bend in the road, so we veered off to the left to follow a short trail back to the Etowah anticipating some sort of natural landmark or a scenic river view.

Just ahead of us, the trail opened into a large flat area cleared of any trees and rocks. A large wooden structure came into view, and as we made our way toward the out-of-place pavilion, I saw a plaque commemorating a Boy Scouts of America troop responsible for the construction.

The pavilion was surprisingly sturdy and very large. A metal roof held up several large poles on the outside of the shelter. Inside, the bottom was covered with a thick layer of relatively fresh gravel.

"This is really cool," Mike said as we walked under to explore a bit further.

As it turned out, the area here was a popular destination for overnight camping trips for local scout troops. The cleared area was large enough to accommodate a sizable number of tents, and the nearby gravel road meant the site was easily accessible but still relatively remote.

We ventured down toward the water and walked along a short trail hugging the riverside before nearly reaching our lunch spot. Turning back, we made it back to the pavilion, heading back to the gravel road to continue back to the car.

Making our way back from the pavilion, I made up rhymes and songs about the forest to entertain Lucy, who at this point was mostly over the trail and the outdoor adventure. So far, we had only seen a bit of river and some wildlife. The WMA trail system was well-worn but not particularly exciting on this side of the river. If we waded through the river, we may have seen some of the more epic sights the WMA had to offer.

Besides the Etowah and the pond we came across early in the day, the attractions and natural locales here were lacking compared to many other destinations in north Georgia where we've recently traveled.

As I sang made-up rhymes and lyrics that were less than mature, a small deer hopped out of the woods to our right and ran off into the distance, stopping a short way away to look back at us.

"I probably shouldn't have been singing so loudly, huh?" I asked somewhat rhetorically from the front of the line. We laughed at the thought of my song scaring away the wildlife.

We made it back to the car with little fanfare a few hours after first stepping into the woods. There were a few more people setting up camps around the parking lot, but many of the horse trailers and trucks were gone by the time we arrived back. We were among the last to leave the WMA.

After packing up and loading everyone into the car, we drove off along the old paved road deeper into the forest to see if we could find any other interesting spots from the comfort of the car. We passed a few old concrete bunkers but nothing truly remarkable stood out.

We continued along the dirt road where we hiked just a few hours earlier and again passed the short trail leading off to the Boy Scout pavilion. With that, we turned our attention to home.

Once we made it back to Atlanta, I read more about the Dawson Forest Wildlife Management Area and found myself wishing I that I had known the lore and history of the WMA before adventuring there. I spent hours that night reading alien conspiracy theories and watching videos online of urban explorers who braved the darkness into some of the flooded underground bunkers looking for whatever the old buildings had hidden away. Looking back, our trip seemed like a waste of potential.

The feeling of an artificial and manmade experience finally made sense. The bunkers were once towering laboratories hidden off in the forest away from prying eyes and curious locals. The forest, long abandoned by Lockheed Martin and the federal government, became purposeless once the experiments were over.

That's why the land was modified to serve as a wildlife management area. That's why the buildings were barricaded away and flooded.

If I had known any of this before venturing off, I would have kept my eyes open for an alien instead of snakes and deer.

Toccoa River & Benton MacKaye Trail Section

IT WAS UNSEASONABLY WARM for January. Following a bit of rain and chilly winds to open the year, the middle of January felt more like a fledgling spring than the dead of winter.

After the rush of the holidays and driving all over the southeastern states to visit family and friends over the Christmas and New Year breaks, it was time to get back to the grind of life. I was looking forward to being outside again after the break from the holidays.

Today was going to be a special day hike, because, for the first time, both my daughter Lucy and my dog Raven would be joining me on the trail. I adopted Raven several months earlier and had taken her on a few short hikes and one full day's hike before planning a larger hike with her and Lucy.

Most mornings, my six-year-old would be the first one out of bed and rummaging in the kitchen for breakfast while I dozed the early hours of the day away. But not this morning. This morning belonged to adventure.

I crashed into Lucy's bedroom just after 7 a.m., turning the lights on and proclaimed that today would be a day of great adventure. My daughter sleeps a lot like I do. Neither of us enjoy a rude awakening to brash songs about hiking and adventure, nor do we like having the lights turned on while we're still under the covers.

The plan for the day was to drive slightly more than two hours north of Atlanta to the Toccoa River Swinging Bridge and hike along the river for as far as our legs and the sun would allow. I recently read a bit about the historic bridge and wanted to see it up close for myself.

For this trip, I planned a special surprise for Lucy. I had recently purchased a new backpacker's propane stove and wanted to test its capabilities in the wilderness. What better to surprise the little one than by cooking up a hot, dehydrated meal by the river for lunch? Today's lunch would be an old favorite: chili mac.

We quickly dressed, grabbed our gear, loaded the car and headed out a little after 8 a.m. in the morning. The conversation during the drive quickly turned to Raven and how we should handle her on the trail.

"Can I hold her leash?" Lucy asked as we made our way to North Georgia's Chattahoochee National Forest in the Jeep.

"Definitely, but we need to make sure that she'll be okay first. So, I'll walk her to start. Fair?"

"Okay," she responded.

I had to know that Raven would behave and be well-mannered on the trail before handing the leash off to Lucy. Unfortunately, the only way that I know to train a dog to hike is to go hiking. So, that's what we did. We were going hiking.

Two or so hours later, we arrived at the old forest road leading to the trailhead. The gravel road here was washed out and filled with massive, muddy divots. After several bumpy moments of driving down into the gorge toward the river valley, we finally arrived at the parking lot. There were only two other cars parked at the bottom. As sociable as I often pretend to be, I would always opt for isolation and quiet in the forest over crowds. For me, the quiet stillness of the forest helps remove me from my daily anchors. Technology, work, chores... those are all supplanted in the forest by my surroundings.

Lucy ran off to pee behind some nearby trees, while I harnessed the dog and gathered the packs as we prepared to set off.

An older couple walked toward us from the trail below the parking lot with their dog as Lucy returned to the car. The man held a hefty camera bag and carried a sturdy tripod over his right shoulder. He must have had 20 pounds of camera gear strapped to his back, more weight than what was currently strapped to mine and Lucy's combined.

We stopped to chat a little about the river and the bridge while our dogs sniffed each other.

"How far down is the bridge?" I asked.

"Not too far at all," the photographer responded, pointing back in the direction where he and his wife had just come. "It's just a few hundred yards down the hill."

"Great," I responded.

The pair wished us luck as we headed off toward the bridge.

The sun shined brightly, drenching the entire canopy above in a warming glow of golden yellow light. Lucy and I brought along jackets, but we quickly stuffed these inside of our packs, instead relying on long shirt sleeves and the sun to keep us comfortable as we set off toward the swinging bridge.

The trees overhead provided a delightful shade while offering short stints of bright sun cracking through the mostly bare limbs above. A light breeze blew through the parking lot, but this did not dampen our collective spirits.

As we hiked to the river, we spotted a large, and well-crafted, campsite off to our left. A father and son were tearing down their temporary home in the woods from the night before, packing their bags and preparing to return to the real world. Their site was only a few yards away from the Toccoa River, which flowed lazily here up to and under the massive swinging bridge. Several impressive fire rings were scattered on the flat landscape down the steep hill from the trail.

"What a fantastic place to camp," I told Lucy. The campsites here provided views of the Toccoa, which sat only a few dozen feet away, and the swinging bridge that towered over the river itself.

As we approached the bridge, the enormity of the manmade structure came into full view. At 270 feet across, the bridge is one of the longest swinging bridges in the country, and it shows. The trail ahead of us ended right at the entrance to the bridge, and Lucy stood in front of it in complete awe as she basked in the remarkable feat of engineering smack in the middle of the wilderness.

The Toccoa River swinging bridge is the main attraction in the area and a popular destination for wildlife and nature photographers throughout the region. Built in 1977 by the USDA Forestry Service along with sponsorship from the Georgia Appalachian Trail Club, the swinging bridge offers picturesque views of the river and surrounding area from high above the waters below.

The bridge is truly a marvel of engineering and is simultaneously perfectly at home and peculiarly out of place against the backdrop of the forest.

Construction of a bridge so far from civilization must have been an impressive undertaking. It would have been impossible to bring a large crane or any kind of heavy machinery down into the river valley from the mountains above, so much of the bridge would have been hand-built.

The apprehension Lucy felt as she stood at the foot of the bridge must have been minuscule compared to what was going through Raven's doggie brain. The dog was not comfortable walking across the bridge in the slightest, and for one of the only times in her life, she walked timidly behind me with her tail between her hind legs as we all crossed as a group instead of plowing ahead from the front where she typically feels most comfortable.

The rocking motion startled me as I made my way onto the bridge, and even my stomach began to sink after a few uneasy steps. I've never been particularly fond of heights, but I put on a brave face and made the best of our situation. We were here. We needed to cross, and I wasn't going to be the reason why we drove two hours only to see the bridge, turn around and go home.

I imagined how many thousands of people had crossed this very bridge before us and how many will step foot on it in the future.

Lucy walked behind me and held my hand as we crossed to the other side. Between us cowered Raven who slowly, but surely, found her footing as we reached the midway point.

The bridge bounced ever so slightly with each step. As tall and as sturdy as the bridge seemed to be from the edge or below, stepping onto it proved that it was not an immovable object. In fact, it was designed to flex and bounce.

Another photographer sat on the opposite bank snapping photos from a large tripod as we approached. I wondered if he caught a glimpse of the three of us walking along the 270-foot suspended platform and thought about asking him for a picture of our small group. I hoped he hadn't captured my apprehension and wobbling knees.

After crossing the bridge, we looked around for a riverside trail that we could follow for a bit before deciding to follow a white diamond blaze up the hill and deeper into the forest. A small stream with even smaller, miniature waterfalls flowed from the hill beside us down into the Toccoa River below.

Ahead of us was the Benton MacKaye Trail, named after the man who conceived the Appalachian Trail itself. The BMT spans nearly 300 miles through Georgia, North Carolina and Tennessee and is widely considered to be one of the premier backpacking trails in the southeast.

I've hiked a few short sections of the Benton MacKaye before, but

I would hardly call myself an expert on the trail or its features. In my mind, it's a lot like the Appalachian Trail in terms of difficulty and general scenery. The BMT even shares many of the same miles of the AT.

The BMT was blazed with a white diamond as opposed to the white rectangle found along the AT. More than 80 miles of the trail can be found in North Georgia, and this was a particularly popular section of the BMT thanks to the swinging bridge.

As we made our way up the hill toward the first diamond blaze, fatigue of the legs came instantaneously. For the first mile or so, a steep elevation gain of nearly a thousand feet stood between us and a more leisurely stroll along the ridgeline above us.

I did not expect such a difficult start to the day, and Lucy suffered as we continued to climb upward from the Toccoa. I did my best to keep a positive outlook and encouraged her to continue whenever she slowed or stopped, but my legs burned, as well. Lucy, like me, could probably hike for 20 miles in a single afternoon along a soft, flat trail. But, also like me, when the elevation becomes steep, Lucy slows to a crawl.

Raven was anxious and confidently led the way up the never-ending incline. Lucy and I would stop every so often to take a drink of water and rest our legs, necessary for both of us. Raven was too excited to spend much time at a standstill and prompted us to keep moving several times if we were still for too long. The dog was loving the hike so far.

Before too long, we crested the ridgeline at the top of the first mountain, feeling accomplished and pleased with our progress, albeit out of breath. The trail here evened out and followed a much smoother, far less strenuous path for the foreseeable future, so we took advantage of the favorable terrain and continued.

We walked for another mile or so until at a much more gingerly pace until we came to a clearing where we took off our packs and marveled at the views below. The fall and winter had long stripped the leaves from the trees surrounding us, showcasing a scenic view of the valley below and accompanying mountain range a few miles away on the opposite side the valley.

Lucy and Raven sat next to a fallen tree and ate an afternoon snack while I wandered off to find a good spot to relieve myself.

Pine trees dotted the landscape and provided a small bit of greenery in an otherwise brown and grey forest. The green valley must have been two thousand feet below us by this point, and the scattered farms and rural houses below felt as though they belonged in a Claude Lorraine painting. The river, more than a mile behind us on the far side of the mountain, was no longer in sight.

Two old logging roads convened at the clearing while the trail continued to the north. If not for the white diamond blaze, it would have been easy to venture off in the wrong direction here. Thankfully, the trail was incredibly well-marked and hikable, at least in this section, without the need of a map or GPS.

After returning from my makeshift forest restroom, I sat down next to Lucy to snack and drink a bit of water.

Once our bellies were full of peanuts, bits of chocolate, jerky and other hiking treats, we set off again along the ridgeline toward Bryson Gap, determined to push as far as we could into the afternoon to make the most of the day's light.

The path remained mostly flat along the next two miles, and the walk along the ridge was peaceful and scenic despite the complete covering of leaves below our feet. The leaves created an icy effect, and since the trail's width along the ridge was thinner than up climb up to the ridge, we were careful to avoid any potential missteps.

Every so often a view of the mountains in the distance or the valley below would appear off to our right through the trees, and we'd stop to take in the sights for a moment or two. Resting was not as necessary for either Lucy or I since there was very little elevation change here, but we occasionally stopped regardless to soak in nature's beauty and gaze off into the distance.

Along the way, we talked about wild animals like boars and bears. Lucy asked about bears, and I told her of my experiences the previous year spotting the creatures in the Great Smoky Mountains National Park. I hoped to not scare Lucy into fearing an attack from a black bear and reassured her that bears were far more interested in eating her beef jerky in the middle of the night than eating her in broad daylight.

"Bears are way more scared of us than we are of them," I told her. "But, we have to keep our eyes open because they are wild animals, and they're unpredictable. You never know what a wild animal will do. So, you always have to pay attention."

"What if it's hungry?" Lucy asked.

"There's a lot of things in the woods for him to eat that are way tastier than you are!"

According to the Georgia Department of Natural Resources Wildlife Resources Division, there are no recorded black bear attacks on humans in Georgia. Ever. As in, no one has ever been seriously threatened by a bear here, much less killed. At least not on record.

Regardless, a respect for nature and her creatures is incredibly important to fully appreciate the wild, even in our own backyards. I've hiked dozens of trails in Georgia, North Carolina, South Carolina and Tennessee, and bear sightings are incredibly rare on the most trafficked footpaths. Still, they can and do happen.

As we continued to discuss the forest's animals, Bryson Gap slowly came into view ahead of us. We rounded a small bend and spotted a makeshift campsite directly in the center of the trail. The camp spot featured a small stone fire ring, and old logs were positioned to provide seating for campers.

The forest was still as we surveyed the surroundings. A sign for a water spring sat at the edge of the campsite stating water was 300 feet off the trail down a small spur trail.

On another day, this would make a fun place to camp.

I threw my pack on the ground next to a log and looked for a place to sit, but the logs were all covered with small termites. This was disappointing since Bryson Gap would have made a good resting and lunch spot if not for the pesky wood-eating bugs crawling all over the place. A campfire and its smoke might have helped, but we didn't plan to stay long enough to start and eventually extinguish a fire.

I encouraged Lucy to drink more water and gave Raven a bowl of water, as well. After a few moments of sitting around on the rocks and resting against the termite-covered logs, it was time to head back. We strapped our packs on and prepped for the hike back to the bridge.

Contrasting the beginning of our day, the walk back from our turnaround point was steady and pleasant. Leaves covered the trail and ground all around us almost like a dusting of light snow, and we steadied our steps during the downhill portions to prevent any slips and falls. Once the trail widened and we were back on top of the ridge, Lucy took the leash and walked Raven back down the mountain.

This was the moment she had been looking forward to the most that day. Her eyes lit up as she held onto Raven's leash, and she walked with a newfound enthusiasm. Raven was aware that Lucy was now her handler and walked along beside her instead of tugging along at the leash as she had done for me earlier in the day. It was nice to see them both enjoying the experience and bonding over the adventure.

We made it back to our resting spot from earlier in the afternoon in the large clearing next to the old logging roads and saw two BMT thru hikers march past us in quick succession as we rested. Neither of them acknowledged us as they passed through the clearing where we again stopped to rest and have a bit of water. I was not completely surprised as the pair carried heavy packs and seemed to be in a hurry to find camp before sunset.

Off in the distance, I heard a faint, familiar song as another hiker approached the clearing.

It was Pink Floyd!

> *The sun is the same in a relative way, but you're older...*
> *Shorter of breath and one day closer to death!*

Another thru hiker came toward us, but this one actually stopped to talk. He was a larger fellow, more than six feet tall with a bulky frame and broad shoulders. He had an impressive beard and wore a bandana on his balding head. He wore hiking boots, dark green cargo shorts and a button up plaid shirt with the top two or three buttons undone. His pack was weathered. He looked legit.

"Great hiking tune," I told the hiker as he stopped to catch his breath and survey the area.

"Oh yeah," he said as he pulled his phone out of his pocket and turned off the music. "I can't hike without music, man."

He was friendly, and we quickly began a conversation about the trail and our gear.

We talked for a while about the Benton MacKaye and his recent thru hike of the Appalachian Trail. Unlike most backpackers, he began the trail at Mount Katahdin in Maine, choosing to hike south instead of north.

"Oh, you're a SOBO," I told him excitedly. He seemed impressed that I knew the thru hiker lingo.

"I just finished in December," he responded. "How's the trail looking ahead?"

"Really smooth. It's almost entirely flat until you get to Bryson Gap. We didn't go any further than that, though." He seemed happy with the news of a few relatively easy miles ahead.

The sun began to dip behind the trees, casting long shadows over the trail and through the forest trees. Despite the unseasonable warmth of the morning and early afternoon, a chill moved over the mountains as shade crept over the forest floor. Dusk seemed to last forever in the Appalachian Mountains, but it brought a definite chill.

We wished our new hiker friend luck and said our goodbyes before heading down the last bit of decline back to the bridge. An hour or so later of mostly uneventful hiking, we met a few other day hikers coming up the hill toward us.

"It looks like it goes on forever," a portly woman said as we approached along on the trail, arms folded and frowning. She didn't seem happy to be climbing the mountain we ascended earlier. I understood exactly how she felt.

"Hey man, how much further does the trail go up?" her husband asked.

"For a while. There's a lot of uphill, but it gets flat and pretty easy once you get to the top," I told him. "It's really pretty up there. The valley below looks like a painting."

The woman huffed and quickly turned around and walked back

down the hill toward the bridge, discouraged at the thought of climbing any further. Her husband turned around and followed her.

"I know how you feel," I told the exhausted woman as we passed the pair on the trail. "It took us a long time to get to the top."

It's in moments like these that I'm particularly impressed with Lucy and her willingness to join me on hikes like these. When all's said and done, she's always right there with me, powering over mountains as though she was born to hike. The hike, especially the beginning of the day, was long and difficult, but she never quit, never gave up. All she needed was water, a few snacks, an excitable puppy and some patient encouragement. It would have been easy to turn around at the first sight of the mountain, give up and walk back to the river to sit the remainder of the day away.

The last bit of our hike took us completely off the ridgeline back down to the river. The sun began to fall behind the nearby mountains, but there was plenty of sunlight left for a bit more enjoyment.

In total, we walked around eight miles before stopping by the river one last time for my late-afternoon dehydrated surprise.

I secured Raven to a tree next to a large outcropping of rocks directly beside the shoreline where she promptly laid down. Lucy hopped onto the river rocks and made her way as far into the water as she could go. I brought out my portable propane stove, connected a fuel canister and began to boil water for our dehydrated meal.

This was a real treat for us. Lucy and I had never eaten a hot meal while day hiking before. Our snacks typically include peanuts, crackers, Lunchables, meat sticks and chocolate. Something hot, especially on a chilly winter's afternoon, was a welcome change to our normal hiking routine.

After a while, Lucy came over to investigate what I was doing. I split the package into two portions, and we both ate our late lunch by the water while other hikers passed behind us, exploring the rocky riverside on their own.

By now, it was the late-afternoon and the sun was almost completely behind the mountains and hills overlooking the river valley. The hills around us were shrouded in the mountain shadows.

We packed up our gear, much to Lucy's dismay, and made our way back to the car before losing whatever light the day had left to give.

Raven fell asleep after only a few moments in the car heading back toward the roadways of civilization. Lucy followed shortly after I navigated the Jeep through a particularly difficult section of washed out and bumpy dirt road. After a few moments of rocking back and forth up a muddy hill, we made it back to the relative safety of the pavement.

On the way home, I couldn't help but feel that our first hike as a trio had been a success.

Waters Creek Trail & Dockery Lake Trail

IT WAS CHILLY. Winter had been unpredictable this year, and it was one of the rare, truly frigid days we experienced so far. Despite the low temperatures, I was determined to get out of the house to tackle a new trail I recently discovered, aptly named Waters Creek.

Located in the Chestatee Wildlife Management Area of the Chattahoochee National Forest, Waters Creek Trail initially appeared to be a relatively short, light hike along Waters Creek culminating with a view of a large and well-known waterfall. This was my kind of hike. I studied the area the week before, because it was somewhat close to my apartment, around an hour and fifteen minutes away, and featured both a decently reviewed hike and a waterfall.

By this point in my weekend adventuring, I've explored many of the most popular local trails to the north of Atlanta. While I have fond memories of many of these places, I almost always prefer to tackle a new challenge than return to an already conquered trail. My biggest enjoyment has always come from the new experience, the fresh sites and the unexpected. I'm often surprised by how many times I discover a hidden gem, an underappreciated trail or network of trails that, for whatever reason, is not as well-traveled or popular as other nearby hikes.

Waterfalls are my favorite natural attraction, and I've spent countless hours in recent years hiking up and down mountains and into gorges to see and photograph them up close. Waters Creek Trail's biggest draw was the waterfall, but from what I had read earlier, the trail network here was worth experiencing, as well, as it indirectly connected to the Appalachian Trail to the north, and offered scenic views of the nearby mountains and hills during the winter months.

Lucy and Raven would also accompany me on this Saturday hike. We spent the first hour or so of the morning having breakfast and packing our gear.

Once we were ready, it was time to head off for the wilderness.

An hour and a half after leaving the apartment that morning, we arrived at the Chestatee Wildlife Management Area.

The Chestatee Wildlife Management Area is more than 25,000 acres of pristine North Georgia Appalachian mountain wilderness located in Lumpkin County and featuring dozens of miles of trails ranging from short jaunts to a section of the Appalachian Trail.

Raven was now familiar with a day on the trail after only a few times hiking alongside me. Excited for what was to come, she bounced around inside of the car as we made our way down an old forest service road toward our ultimate destination.

We arrived at the trailhead around 11 that morning and drove past a U.S. Forest Ranger as we found the gravel parking lot leading to the trailhead. I stopped at the information board, looking for any references to parking or daily use fees, but there were none.

We parked next to two other cars and strapped on our packs, ready to take on the day.

There was no trail here, at least, not the typical trail that I've hiked in recent years in these parts. The trail that I read about in preparing for the hike, was a continuation of the forest service road that was closed to vehicles, presumably for the winter, but perhaps permanently, and not a real hiking trail at all. Further up the mountain, the road connected with a more traditional trail far above the river and scattered campsites below, but it would take a mile or two and perhaps an hour or more to reach it.

Like most of the forest service roads I'd come across in Appalachia, this one was a mixture of washed out gravel and dirt, with uneven bumps and potholes scattered throughout. The road was mostly dry, which was a pleasant departure from some of the recent hikes, where mud and dirty water were everywhere.

After checking the map and finding our bearings, we set off down the road to see what we could find.

Our trio walked along Waters Creek Road for a mile or so, until we came to our first landmark: a campsite. There would be eleven campsites in total, A through K, along the hike and as we quickly noticed, each one offered a slightly different camping experience than the others around them. Each was far enough away from the others to offer a bit of privacy and solitude.

Camping was restricted to these eleven campsites only, and there were plenty of signs and markers along the creek warning potential would-be campers to set up camp elsewhere. Many of what I thought were the best spots along the river were prohibited, presumably to keep backpackers and campers from trashing the sites directly beside the creek. Each campsite came with a very visible 14-day limit sign on camping at the same place. I wondered if anyone had ever tested that law.

None of the sites held occupants. Maybe it was too cold or too early in the day. Regardless, we pushed on along the mostly flat riverside road, stopping every so often to take in the views and check out the shallow creek beside us.

Much of the land on the opposite side of the creek was private property, and the owners made sure everyone in the forest knew to stay off their land and to abstain from fishing the creek waters. Signs, warning against fishing and trespassing, were carefully placed a few yards apart along an inconsistent barbed wire fence. These continued beside the creek along much of the road.

A short while into the day, I noticed a nearby mountain off to our right, covered in massive boulders that jutted out from the side of the hill. The rocks were gigantic, but they appeared to be climbable all the way to the very top of the mountain.

Lucy and I marveled at the splendor off in the distance. The boulders were no more than 100 yards or so away from the road below, and a slight incline away from the road offered a clear view of the naturally made structure.

Playing and scrambling around on the rocks would have made for an enjoyable afternoon, but, from the looks of it, neither Lucy nor Raven would be able to climb very high. The boulders were massive.

Climbing these rocks might have proven impossible for me, as well, but I would have relished the opportunity to give it a try.

"We'll come back and check it out if we have time," I told Lucy as we pressed on down the road.

Eventually, as we approached a water crossing over a small, paved section of the forest road, we heard voices in the distance. I spotted a pair of men with two dogs, slightly off the trail, and waved to them as we approached.

"Good morning," I greeted them as we walked past. Both men carried large, bulging packs with enough gear for a weekend or more in the woods. "Have y'all made it up to the falls yet?"

"Nah, we just got here," one of the men responded with a massive grin. He seemed excited to be in the woods. They must have arrived shortly before us in one of the two cars spotted back at the parking lot.

The pair was standing across from campsite D, which was situated next to a beautiful rocky stream flowing down into Waters Creek from the hillside above. The campsite was idyllic and my favorite so far. Perhaps they were defending it from us or other potential campsite suitors.

"This is a great spot," I told the pair as I surveyed the surrounding area. "If I were camping, this is where I'd stay." Both nodded in agreement. They seemed relieved that we were not staying the night.

We exchanged pleasantries for a few more moments before

Raven's jumping and whining forced us to move on ahead. As good as she'd been on the trail during her first few hikes, Raven still had the tendency to act overly excitable while meeting other dogs. When that happens, I've found it best to keep moving and to hope the distraction fades from her short-term memory. Once we put boot to ground for a few paces, she had no issues settling back into the flow of the hike.

We began a slight climb in elevation as the road diverted from the creek and moved up the mountain. The hike became more intense here, and we stopped often to rest our legs. Eventually, the road ended and gave way to a proper trail, much thinner in width and softer on the feet.

We passed all the designated campsites as we made our way to the end of the Waters Creek Trail. Lucy scurried off behind some nearby bushes to use the restroom while Raven and I waited patiently on the trail, scouting for any passersby.

Around two and a half miles into the day, we reached a junction with the Dockery Lake Trail, which ran from the Dockery Lake Campgrounds all the way to the Appalachian Trail, climbing some 2,000 feet along the way.

We met the Dockery Creek Trail somewhere in the middle between the campgrounds below and the Appalachian Trail above. Unsure of how close we were to the AT, I decided to press on and add another few hours to our hike since it was still relatively early in the day and we had made good time so far.

The trail beneath of our feet felt like am actual trail and not just some abandoned forest service road, which rejuvenated me.

"We're going to climb a mountain!" I told Lucy excitedly as we marched onward.

Her response was a more sheepish than I hoped.

"I want to go back," she said. "I don't like heights."

I imagined she was picturing a scene from Sylvester Stallone's "Cliffhanger" and not a leisurely walk along a proven mountain hiking trail far away from anything resembling an edge or drop-off. Eventually, I convinced her to move on after promising better mountain views from the ridges above. The mountain here gently sloped back down to the valley below.

"We're not going to climb a mountain," I told her reassuringly. "We're just walking up a trail."

The trail here was overgrown with tall grass and saplings that encroached on the footpath. Leaves from the oaks above covered the forest floor, as well. The Dockery Lake Trail did not seem to be a popular choice for day hikers. In fact, we did not see anyone, all day, besides the two backpackers at the start of the Waters Creek Trail some three miles earlier.

The sense of isolation soon took hold as we made our way further from the creek back down the mountain.

Despite the overgrowth from below and the constant uphill, the trail was quite scenic. The leafless trees provided deep views into the valley floors below.

Every so often, an opening would appear on the ridge, displaying the full breadth of the mountains and hills surrounding us. A few of these mountains must have been 4,000 or more feet tall.

As we moved higher through the forest, a small clearing opened in front of us under a pleasant covering from the trees above. Massive rocks were exposed on the ground, offering a bit of flat space to sit and rest. The rocks were surrounded by trees on both sides of the trail, providing a bit of relief from the cold winds while the sun was able to poke through to provide small spots of bright warmth.

"Let's stop and eat lunch here," I told Lucy after surveying the clearing. Despite indulging in a snack a short while earlier during a bathroom break, we were both excited to fill our bellies and rest our legs for a while. The last bit of hiking was a non-stop uphill marathon, and it appeared as though the trail moving forward would mostly keep us on an incline, as well.

I wrapped Raven's leash around a small tree while Lucy rummaged through her pack deciding which snack to eat first. For this hike, she had brought a variety of snacks, including our now-staple Lunchables. I poured Raven a cup of her food, which she immediately chowed down.

I also brought a few snacks, including a couple of beef jerky sticks, my own Lunchables and two slices of leftover pizza from the previous night's dinner. I decided on the pizza, even though the pepperonis had been picked off by a nefarious pepperoni thief the night before.

We heard the distant hum of an overhead plane as it moved closer to us and eventually passed just a few hundred feet above our heads below the clouds flying off to the east.

"The people on that plane are the closest people to us right now," I told Lucy as we munched our snacks.

Eventually, it was time to continue. We repacked our bags, grabbed our trash, drank a bit more water and continued onward toward the AT.

After a lengthy section of relatively flat trail, we came to a small stream where a fallen tree provided a challenging way across. I decided to go first. After a bit of coercion, Raven hopped on the fallen tree and followed closely behind as I made my way over.

Lucy watched us carefully and hesitated, but eventually climbed onto the tree as well. Slowly, and cautiously, she made her way across by placing one short step in front of another.

"I'm not going to make it!" she said as she wobbled, then steadied herself.

"You've got it!" I encouraged her.

A few seconds later, she was far enough across to hop down onto the sandy bank of the stream. I could not have been prouder. In truth, the fallen tree was only a foot or two above the shallow creek, but the challenge of crossing using the tree as a plank instead of rock hopping was the perfect representation of the kind of experiences I wanted to share with my daughter whenever we ventured off into the woods. It's always been moments like that where I've felt most proud of her.

"Good job! You're a trail killer!"

"You can't kill a trail dad," Lucy sarcastically quipped in response. That, too, was the perfect representation of our experiences on the trail.

Lucy had spent a lot of time hiking with me over the last year. I thought hiking together would be a healthy hobby that we could both enjoy and something that we could do on our weekends together to bond. Hiking had become one of my favorite hobbies in recent years, and I wanted to share my enthusiasm.

While fatigue and tired legs get in her way as often as they do mine, and do their part to dampen the mood, Lucy is always willing to go on an adventure to the woods with her dad, even knowing that these adventures mean challenging work.

Our group continued up the mountain, sights now set on reaching the AT junction before the afternoon sun began to dip back behind the tall Appalachian hills. Coming back down the mountain would be much easier than climbing up had been earlier in the day. The trail was not steep, but the upward incline was never-ending. Coming the other way, entirely downhill, would be a relative breeze in comparison.

We marched on. The trail continued to slowly climb, without an end in sight. I had no idea how far away we were from the AT, but it felt as though we had hiked for hours on this small stretch of upward path. I looked at my GPS to see where we were, but the Dockery Lake Trail was not marked on the map. We were simply a blue dot against a green backdrop in the middle of a literal nowhere. The AT was not too far ahead, so we pushed on, not entirely knowing what we would find once we reached our destination.

On and on we climbed. Even Raven slowed and walked beside me instead of pulling me along from the front of the line.

After what seemed like an entire day hiking just a half mile, we reached the junction of the AT. I expected some kind of sight or worthwhile view from the top of the ridge, but there was nothing outside of a small wooden sign directing us back down the mountain from where we had come. We sat in the afternoon sun for a long while, resting and talking about the woods, animals and hikers.

The sun began to fall back onto the horizon and a chill crept over the forest as we rested. In truth, the journey to the Appalachian Trail was a bit lackluster. If there were more time, we could have hiked a bit more of the AT or even stayed on the trail overnight.

As the cold winds turned toward us, we quickly made our way back down the mountain and toward the car. The hike back was uneventful. Our pace was much quicker since we stopped far less frequently, thanks to continuous downhill hike.

We crossed the same downed tree over the stream as before, and Lucy was excited to walk over the log the second time around. We pushed on down the mountain back toward Waters Creek, making excellent time in our race against the setting sun.

A short while later, we were back on the gravel road, walking past the lettered campsites from earlier in the day until we finally made it back to the parking lot.

We stopped at the car and dropped off our packs. I took Raven to a small grassy area next to the creek in hopes that she would pee before the drive home. Lucy played by the water as the sun faded completely behind the nearby hills and dusk overtook the forest.

I was exhausted and felt defeated as we finally loaded into the car. We had hiked more than eight miles along Waters Creek Trail and Dockery Lake Trail toward the AT and back, but the day felt incomplete without seeing the falls.

We had come here for the specific purpose of seeing that waterfall, but I didn't want to let the missed site ruin an otherwise perfectly good day. While there had been plenty interesting sights along the way, particularly the views from the ridgeline, it was hard to put a happy face on the day without finishing what we had started. Dealing with sore legs, tired feet and exhaustion have always been much easier to handle when accompanied by the memory of a majestic ridgeline view or a waterfall.

We loaded into the Jeep, and Raven immediately curled into a little fuzz ball in the back seat, falling fast asleep next to Lucy in a matter of moments. Of the three of us, she was the most physically exhausted. I started the car, and we made our way back down the forest service road toward home.

Suddenly, there it was! Off to our right, back toward the river was a massive waterfall. I stopped the Jeep and looked out of the passenger side window toward the rushing water falling over the black rock. The river was below us only a few feet away, and the view here was stunning.

"How did we miss this?" I asked Lucy. "It was right by the parking lot the whole time! How did we miss this?"

No wonder the waterfall was a popular recommendation on the internet! We shared a good laugh as we drove home.

Our day was complete after all.

Panther Creek Falls Trail

WEATHER, TIME AND ANY NUMBER of circumstances force us to make do with what's available or to accept a change of plans. This has always been especially true for hiking and backpacking.

I've learned that even the best researched and well thought out adventures rarely go exactly as intended.

Out on the trail, despite my best planning, I've found myself "winging it" more times than I can remember, even though I knew exactly what I wanted to do and see before setting off. Rain, fallen trees that obstruct substantial portions of the trail, missing signs and unexpected turns have often forced me to improvise, abandon plans or formulate a new strategy on the fly.

My original plan for the day was to drive nearly two hours from my North Atlanta apartment to Fort Mountain State Park and tackle the 8.2-mile Gahuti Loop Trail with my daughter. But, after waking up in the early morning and checking the weather reports, a day filled with soggy, muggy and generally wet conditions was not at all appealing. Rain was forecast in the area for much of the day, but staying home felt like a waste of an otherwise perfectly good weekend day.

I scanned the weather reports for the northwest, the northeast and even to the south of Atlanta, where I rarely hike, to find a suitable place to enjoy warm, dry weather and finally decided on an old favorite: Panther Creek Falls Trail. The rain would eventually make it there as well, but not until the late afternoon, hopefully long after we were on our way home.

The Gahuti Trail would have to wait for another weekend.

Panther Creek is a wildly popular choice for day hikers in the metro Atlanta area as it's only about an hour and a half north of the city in Turnerville, Georgia and features one of the state's most scenic waterfalls. The trail itself is a relatively short seven or so miles out and back (officially), but I've found that the trail is a mile or so longer in total than what's advertised. My pedometer has never stopped at seven miles before reaching the car at the end of the day.

Due to the convenience of its location and the natural beauty found there, Panther Creek is filled with hikers looking to escape the daily grind with a day in the woods, even on the coldest days. Today was chilly, but the afternoon promised a bit of warmth before the late afternoon rain arrived.

This would be my third hike of Panther Creek. I almost always prefer isolation over crowds, but Panther Creek is well-worn for a reason. The trail is beautiful and the hike is not too laborious for anyone experienced and in somewhat decent physical shape.

As we dressed and ate breakfast, I debated whether to bring Raven. She had done well on her first few hikes, but due to the crowds, taking her today would mean constant vigilance, profuse apologies any time she jumped on someone and the worry of someone taking offense to my overly-friendly pup.

As good as she'd been on the trails so far, we'd encountered only a handful of other hikers and even fewer dogs to truly test her temperament while hiking. Panther Creek would have more dogs and people in the first mile than she had seen on all her previous hikes with us combined.

I put her in her crate before we prepared to leave, but a last-minute change of heart saw Raven hop into the car with Lucy and I as we headed off to the trail. It felt wrong to leave her behind, even just for the day. I decided to suck it up and deal with my responsibility as a dog owner and braced myself for the upcoming awkwardness a mischievous dog always brings.

We set off toward Turnersville, driving up I-985 to the northeast of Atlanta, leaving just after nine that morning.

The drive to the trailhead was uneventful and familiar. Heading up the interstate toward Tallulah Gorge and the northeast Georgia mountains was commonplace for us. Not only was this the area where we'd done most of our recent hiking, it was also the same road we routinely travel to go to the family farm in upstate South Carolina where we spend the occasional weekend experiencing a more simple and relaxed life.

After a quick stop for gas and to buy a few extra goodies for the trail, we arrived at the trailhead about an hour and a half after leaving home, turning into the parking lot shortly before 11 in the morning. Many cars and Jeeps filled the parking lot, and the sun was cutting through the trees overhead offering a bit of warmth on an otherwise chilly day.

I stopped by the information board to pick up our parking permit before heading off down the trail, slipping a five-dollar bill into a permit envelope and sending Lucy back up to the registration box to deposit our fee.

A small stream ran beside the parking lot here. A picnic table and a restroom facility were also nearby. These amenities at the trailhead were uncommon for us. A bathroom was a real treat, even if it smelled like a sewage processing plant on a hot summer's afternoon.

After gearing up, we set off toward the falls crossing underneath US 23, a four-lane continuation of I-985, from the parking lot to the north. Several large pieces of graffiti were on full display under the bridge here, some far cleverer than others. Much like carvings on shelters or sidewalk street art, the better the quality, the less I seem to be offended by its presence.

Lucy held Raven's leash as we set off, both excited to be back on the trail.

Lucy and I had hiked Panther Creek the year before with a few friends. I was surprised by her memory of the day as she rattled off details and asked questions about the trail.

"Is the big rock still there?" she asked.

"Of course. It would take an awful lot to move those boulders"

"Can we eat lunch there again?"

"Definitely."

During our last trip, our group had stopped on the river's edge and climbed a massive boulder hanging over the water to have a quick snack. That moment had been Lucy's favorite of the day, and I wanted to make sure that we could have the same experience again.

As we made our way further from the parking lot, the sound of cars and trucks from the highway faded behind the wooded hills. We quickly passed a young couple carrying out their gear from the night before.

The young girl carried a large sleeping bag while her boyfriend walked behind her carrying a backpack filled to the brim with an overnighter's necessities and possibly a bit more.

The first mile or so of the trail followed high above Panther Creek but gradually worked its way into the valley below, dropping several hundred feet in elevation as the path approached the water.

Eventually, the first of three small wooden bridges appeared before us, foreshadowing more than a mile of flat riverside hiking, the most scenic stretch of the riverside trail. The elevation leveled here and became much more manageable for Lucy and Raven as the roots and rock from above gave way to a soft, sandy path below our feet. The sand and loose stones suggested that, at some point in time, every part of the valley had once served as the riverbed for Panther Creek.

In addition to its popularity as a day hiking destination, campers also flock to Panther Creek. It's not uncommon to see the occasional Boy Scout troop or group of weekend adventurers setting up camp all along the upper portions of the river.

Several campsites dotted the riverbank in this flat section, some larger and more elaborate than others. One of the first sites we passed featured an old reclining living room chair dumped inside it. It must have taken a herculean effort to bring that heavy chair to the waterside.

"What is that?" Lucy asked as we pushed down the trail.

"It looks like a chair," I responded. "How in the world did that get down here?" I wondered why anyone would make such an effort to trash the area. It must have seemed like a fantastic idea to bring the old La-Z-Boy down into the gorge, but taking it back out was never on the agenda.

Overuse of the trail is a genuine problem at Panther Creek. It's been said that the trail is being "loved to death," an apt description of the conditions here. Though mostly clean and free from overt trash like scattered beer cans and cigarette butts, random leftovers from campers and hikers are not uncommon. If a recliner found its way into the valley, who knows what else has been pulled out from the campsites over the years?

Like other areas we'd hiked recently, Panther Creek could soon become a candidate for a ban on overnight camping, particularly close to the falls.

I've always instilled in Lucy the importance of packing out our trash. Those lessons even extend to bagging up Raven's excrement, which she dutifully carries out on her own back. Each of us carries our own small, plastic grocery bags for trash. Raven carries a handful of small doggie bags. If needed, these bags, both Raven's and ours, are tied to the outside of our packs.

Shortly after passing the recliner, we arrived at the large boulder hanging off the river's shore where we had snacked and rested on our last trip to Panther Creek.

Next to the boulder was a fantastic campsite claimed by another young couple. A hammock and small dome tent were set beside one another, both overlooking a serene section of flowing, rocky river. This was the most idealistic campsite we had come across yet, though it was a bit too close to the trail for my liking. Still, during the evening and overnight, it would have been immensely peaceful lying just a few feet away from the white-capped rushing water.

Several large boulders were scattered throughout the riverside clearing. A few, such as our lunch spot, were positioned next to or half-way into the water, which was 10 or so feet below the top of the boulder.

"Is this it?" Lucy asked excitedly.

"It sure is! Go ahead and take off your pack. I'll help you up."

We had hiked no more than two miles by this point, but I welcomed a break and the opportunity to once again rest at this unique spot. Our hike was a leisurely one, and we had more than enough time to relax before the afternoon rains.

I helped Lucy to the top of the boulder and handed her the dog. It would be a bit more difficult for me to get on top of the rock, however.

I resorted to extending my hiking pole to its longest length and crawled somewhat embarrassingly up to the top of the boulder on my protruding stomach using my pole to steady myself. Once I made it to the top, I looked around to make sure no one had seen the uncoordinated spectacle. It had not been a dignified climb, but I had made it to the top nonetheless.

We sat on the rock next to the river for a while, eating and watching the passersby hiking to and from the falls downriver. Many groups, large and small, came and went while we relaxed. Raven ate a cup of dog food while Lucy had a Lunchables. I snacked on peanuts and chocolate and drank water.

After eating, we hopped back onto the trail and made our way down the last mile or so before the falls. The trail here climbed onto rock and featured a wire railing, offering a flimsy barrier from a possible fall, but despite the safety precautions, this section of trail is infamously difficult and even deadly.

In 2015, 23-year old John-Michael Ritchey fell to his death from these very rocks. Ritchey, a teacher, and his wife were hiking with another couple when he fell from the path above the river, hitting his head on a rock below. Injuries, and even Ritchey's accident, reinforce the need for constant caution when wilderness adventuring. It only takes one misplaced step in the woods to seriously injure yourself. No matter how experienced the adventurer, accidents and injuries can happen to anyone.

Hikers often fear bears, snakes and creepy crawlers while out on the trail, but the truth is that most of the accidents that happen in the forest are physical injuries.

A twisted ankle, a broken leg, fatigue, burns, falling, heat stroke and dehydration are far more common than snakebites or bear attacks in North Georgia.

I urged Lucy to stay to the far right of the path, as close to the rock face as possible, and to watch her footing carefully. Thankfully, the rocks were mostly dry, though patches of wet mud required steadfast footing and concentration. Many hikers have misjudged the difficulty here, and once on the rocks above the falls, they either stop or turn around to head back toward the safer section of trail after realizing just how perilous the final stretch of trail can be. This causes issues for hikers coming up the trail, as Lucy and I soon discovered.

A few moments on the rocks and Lucy was anxious to get down to the falls. The final stretch of climbing along the rock toward the river below was in front of us, and I could not help but think of the last time that we were here. Lucy had been hesitant and not-at-all sure about her footing. She was more confident now, hopping from rock to rock, sliding down on her butt from layer to layer, and moving with ease down the steep hill.

Ahead of us was a trio of day hikers, including a woman who was obviously uncomfortable walking along the rocks. After crowding behind them for a few feet, we stopped to let them move ahead a bit, but they were painfully slow.

A few moments later, it seemed they barely moved at all. Lucy and Raven were impatient. I struggled to keep Raven from crawling under the feet of the poor woman ahead of us while maintaining my own balance.

She and her husband were at an impasse. Eventually, the pair moved over to let us pass, and within a few seconds, we climbed down the ridge to the water below. Lucy immediately ran over to the sandy beach as Raven and I skipped down a shortcut on the hill, bypassing the final few feet of the trail. Looking back, I saw the woman give up and dejectedly head back out.

"Can I take off my shoes and get in the water?" Lucy asked as Raven and I approached on the sandy beach.

"Sure, but don't get your butt wet," I warned. The water was cold, but it seemed an appropriate payoff for making it to the falls.

Dropping her pack by a long-felled tree, Lucy stripped off her socks and shoes before wading into the freezing river. I stuck my hands in the water to feel. It may have been over 70 degrees outside with a bright and beaming sun, but the water was numbingly frigid.

"I'm going to go hang up the hammock," I said to Lucy after a few moments of taking photos from my phone of her, Raven and the falls. I left her with Raven and walked back away from the river toward the trees. Turning back, I saw the pair standing silently in the water, facing the falls.

The base of the waterfall could have been an advertisement for a hammock company. There were more than a half dozen hanging among the trees as I scouted a space to hang my own. I found a suitable spot in the shade and got to work. A couple next to me asked if I would take a picture of them in their hammock, which I willingly obliged. They seemed happy.

I stepped off two trees that were about 15 feet apart and wrapped my suspension straps around the trunks making sure not to set up too close to another person.

Bringing the hammock along was a good idea and not one that was uniquely my own. I relaxed, swaying in the wind for a while before Lucy came over, asking if she could join. We dried off her feet, and she climbed in to soak up the afternoon sun, while Raven sat on the ground next to us.

We swayed in the warm breeze, our bare feet hanging over the hammock's edge, for a long while.

Around 2:30 in the afternoon, I decided it was time to head back. I packed up the hammock and said goodbye to our hanging neighbors while Lucy played in the water for a few last moments before it was time to trek out of the valley back to the Jeep. Since the path up the rock face was tight and narrow, we waited until there were no other hikers coming down before heading off. The climb out was slow, but we eventually made it back to the sandy, riverside trail without incident.

Lucy, holding Raven's leash, slipped into one of the many streams on the way out, soaking her socks and shoes. After a few minutes of complaining, she eventually changed her attitude and accepted the soggy feet and even made a point to walk through the streams that we would have otherwise avoided. There's a reason why we always wore hiking shoes and brought an extra pair of socks on each hike. Lucy, however, refused to change them.

Our group stopped about halfway back and sat by a small stream for a few moments to have a snack and one final break before the last stretch of inclined trail. Lucy offered to take a photo of Raven and me on a small wooden bridge crossing a creek and I happily agreed. Raven and I posed against the railing, smiling.

The last time Lucy and I hiked Panther Creek, she had struggled on the final uphill push toward the tail end of the trail where the path climbed back out of the valley toward the parking lot on the opposite side of the highway.

But this hike was different.

We stopped to take a few occasional water and rest breaks, but Lucy was much more comfortable hiking up the nearly 1,000 feet of elevation gain than she was a year earlier. I offered encouragement and stopped whenever she needed a break.

We settled into our pace and walked between two couples who were also on the final stretch of uphill. I made a competition out of staying ahead of the other hikers to help encourage Lucy to keep moving.

As we approached the parking lot, I made sure to congratulate and offer a final finish-line high-five to both Lucy and Raven.

"Good job," I told her as we approached the Panther Creek trailhead sign.

"Thanks," she responded, exhausted.

We slowly walked back to the car. Lucy took off her wet shoes while Raven closed her eyes and curled into a little ball of exhausted fur on the backseat next to her.

One last check of the pedometer showed an eight-mile round trip in just over five hours.

Lucy's improvement and comfort on the trail had grown so much in the last year, and it was a joy to watch her gain confidence and strength. Seeing her tackle Panther Creek for the second time gave me the opportunity to directly compare her progress.

Every time we've hiked, she's become more confident, better able to handle the physical challenge and was more willing to put in the work for the reward.

It was another good day and a fantastic hike.

Coosa Backcountry Trail & Duncan Ridge Trail

VOGEL STATE PARK, founded in 1931 around the genesis of the Georgia State Park system, is one of Georgia's oldest and most historically significant state parks. According to the Georgia Department of Natural Resources State Parks and Historic Sites division, the land that is now Vogel once belonged to Fred and Augustus Vogel, a pair of brothers and leather-makers from Milwaukee, Wisconsin.

The Vogel brothers shipped bark harvested from Georgia oak and hemlock trees back to their Wisconsin facilities to be used as part of a leather tanning process. In the early 1900s, a synthetic method was developed to tan leather, and the land and resources from Georgia were no longer necessary to expand the family's business. The Vogel family donated the land that now comprises much of the park to the state in 1927.

Before the Vogels, Native Americans of the Cherokee and Creek tribes long settled and hunted here. Much of that history has been lost to time, but the legacy of the native peoples will forever be tied to the mountains of North Georgia and the Appalachian region.

At just 233 acres, Vogel State Park is one of the state's smallest parks by land area, but one of the grandest in terms of historical significance. Work began in the early 1930s to transform the mountain land into a state park, utilizing workers with the New Deal-era Civilian Conservation Corps (CCC) program. The CCC program was designed to put unmarried, unemployed young men to work during the Great Depression and was instrumental in completing projects, like Vogel State Park, across the depressed United States. Many of the southeast's state parks were constructed during this time utilizing men from this program.

Today, Vogel features a variety of activities for families, hikers and backpackers. Lake Trahlyta, a scenic 22-acre mountain lake, is prominently featured here and arguably the park's most recognizable asset. A handful of waterfalls, campsites and even mini-golf are also available at the park for visitors to enjoy year-round.

Our experience with Vogel came on a cold and wet weekend in late February. We planned to hike the Coosa Backcountry Trail, a 12.9-mile mountain loop that began in the park and continued into the Blood Mountain Wilderness Area of the Chattahoochee National Forest to the north. The trail eventually circled back around, returning to Vogel from the southwest. The goal of the hike was to camp Saturday night on top of Coosa Bald, one of Georgia's 10 highest peaks and one of the state's most underrated summits, and to finish the weekend hike early Sunday afternoon before heading back to Atlanta.

As the state's 10th tallest mountain by elevation, we knew there was a full day of work ahead of us to make it to the top of Coosa Bald, some seven miles down the trail, before the early-evening sunset.

The elevation profile previewed a relatively easy morning with a slight uphill section, followed by a bit of downhill and ending with a four-mile moderately strenuous climb to the top of the mountain to end the day.

The CBT would intersect with the lesser-known but extremely strenuous Duncan Ridge Trail close to Coosa Bald and even featured an approach trail to Blood Mountain, the highest point along the Appalachian Trail in Georgia at 4,458 feet. We would skirt Blood Mountain while utilizing the Duncan Ridge Trail to ascend Coosa.

Another Vogel trail, Bear Hair Gap Trail, could also be accessed from the CBT. We hoped to finish the loop via the Bear Hair Gap Trail on our second day if time allowed.

Many hikers have compared the conditions of the CBT to those commonly found on the Georgia section of the AT thanks to the seemingly never-ending elevation gains and similar terrain. Because of these conditions, some hikers and backpackers have used the CBT as a preparation hike for their AT thru hikes.

Hikers tackling Vogel's trails would find one of Georgia's highest parks by elevation. Coosa Bald, our planned destination, was officially tagged at 4,280 feet by the United States Geological Survey in 1934.

This was a big hike for us.

Not only was this Lucy's first overnight backpacking trip, it was the first time my dog Raven would sleep in the woods overnight, as well.

We would be joined by my friend Jeremy and his dog Prince of Darkness. Prince, an Australian Shepard, was roughly the same age as Raven, just as rambunctious and excitable on the trail.

Jeremy and I backpacked together through the Smokes a year earlier, and this was our first overnight trip together since. Jeremy was tall at just over six feet, impressively tattooed and the kind of scruffy that would often draw the gaze of even the most happily married woman. He was an experienced hiker and backpacker in his own right.

We first met at work, where we bonded over a mutual sense of humor and an appreciation for the off-site lunch. We quickly became friends outside of the office and found ourselves spending the occasional weekend hiking together.

For this adventure, I was carrying my Osprey Atmos 65 AG backpack. This was my second Atmos pack, obtained after my first pack suffered a handful of fabric tears on the previously mentioned trip to the Smokies. I loved my old pack, but its condition made it mostly unusable on the trail. The pack had been responsible for my trail name, Swiss Cheese. I was sentimental.

The new Atmos bag came with an updated suspension system that made carrying around its contents substantially more comfortable on the hips and shoulders than the previous generation's version, and I was looking forward to putting it through its paces for the first time.

Inside of the pack, I carried my REI Lumens 20 degree sleeping bag, an Alps Mountaineering Zephyr 1 tent, four liters of water, filtration, snacks and meals for two days (and two people), my cook kit, a few electronics, and some extra clothes.

I also packed my hammock, a tarp and rope in hopes of being able to hang it at camp once we arrived. In total, I guessed my pack weight to be somewhere around 30 pounds, which was a bit more than I would typically carry thanks to the extra water, my hammock setup and Lucy's food. I packed the night before our departure, and despite the extra weight, the pack fit comfortably against my back thanks to the updated suspension system.

Lucy would carry her Deuter Climber Pack overnight for the first time. Her bag was a 22-liter pack that was just big enough for her winter sleeping bag and a change of clothes. She also insisted on bringing her blanket, which added a bit more weight to her pack. I carried her snacks, meals and water.

In total, Lucy's pack weighed around five pounds, which was a pound or so more than I wanted her to strap to her back. Because we were hiking during the winter, her sleeping bag was fluffier than a summer bag would have been and took up more space than a slimmer, lighter summer bag.

Lucy insisted on bringing a few extras, like the blanket and a few small trinkets, knowing that she would be responsible for the weight on her back. I told her to take mindful consideration of the weight, but my arguments proved fruitless. Lucy had also wanted to carry her food and water. I refused.

Jeremy carried a Deuter backpack, somewhere between 65 and 70 liters in capacity. He packed away his tent, food, water and a few other essential and not-so-essential items for the trip.

I watched the weather closely the week leading up to the trip. As the days ticked off, the chance of sustained rains increased bit by bit every day. On that Monday, there was a 20 percent chance of morning showers. By Friday, it was nearly 100 percent chance of rain Saturday morning, but the weather reports indicated a cloudy, but dry, afternoon and evening. Our second day, Sunday, was projected to be clear, sunny and warm beginning around noon after a slight chance of drizzles in the early morning.

I stubbornly refused to reschedule, despite the threat of rain. We could handle a few hours of the wet.

Lucy and I organized our packs the night before, carefully pouring over the contents to ensure that nothing important was left behind and went to bed early, eagerly anticipating the day to come.

***

I woke up just before 7 a.m. the next morning, excited to begin the day. I took Raven for a quick morning walk and the two of us barged into Lucy's room to rouse her awake. After a few minutes, and several dog licks later, Lucy was out of bed and getting ready for the day.

After showering and finalizing the last bit of gear for the trip, we waited on Jeremy and Prince, who showed up right at our planned meeting time of 7:45 a.m. We loaded our gear and climbed into the Jeep, setting off from my apartment just north of Atlanta a little after 8 a.m.

We arrived at Vogel State Park just after 10 in the morning. Leaving Jeremy and Lucy with the dogs in the car, I went into the visitor center to grab our parking pass and to see if the park's rangers had any advice or suggestions for the hike.

The visitor center contained a small gift shop complete with children's toys, miscellaneous camping and backpacking supplies, Vogel memorabilia and snacks. There were a handful of people in the shop, and a few other backpackers were in line ahead of me grabbing their passes, as well.

I waited in line for a few moments before it was my turn to approach the counter.

"Hi there, I need three backcountry passes," I told an elderly female park ranger.

"How many in your group?" the park ranger asked.

"Three," I responded enthusiastically. "Two adults and one child. Well, five if you count the dogs."

"Five bucks."

That's cheap, I thought. As it turned out, hiking was free. Parking overnight, on the other hand, was a paltry five dollars. I paid the fee and asked the ranger about passes to display on our packs, which I read about online ahead of the trip.

"People ask about those all the time, but we don't give 'em out," she responded.

This was disappointing. I had hoped to get some sort of badge or memento from the park to collect, and I thought Lucy might like having something to hang from her new pack, too.

The park required a detailed itinerary and extensive personal information in case of emergency. After completing a simple form, the ranger gave me a map that was surprisingly rich with detail. Water sources, campsites and other attractions like waterfalls and stream crossings were all clearly marked on the park-supplied map that extended far beyond the borders of the park. Resources like these are one of the benefits provided by state parks that are not often afforded to hikers and backpackers who venture into wilderness areas and national forests.

I grabbed our parking pass and map before making my way back to the car to find a parking space.

A light drizzle began to fall as we removed the netting and pulled our packs from the Jeep's roof rack. Lucy and I wrapped our packs in their waterproof pack covers and strapped ourselves in. Jeremy typically hiked without a cover and did not bring one this weekend, instead relying on a waterproof trash compactor bag inside of his pack to keep his belongings dry. Lucy and I also had trash compactor bags inside of our packs, but both of our bags had their own rain cover.

Up until this point in the morning, we had been mostly free from rain, and we found it foreboding that the drizzles came within moments of stepping off for the trail.

Jeremy and Prince led the way along a paved park road toward the trailhead while Lucy, Raven and I followed behind. Both dogs bounced with excitement as we passed by several not-very-remote campsites close to the visitor's center. A short while later, we turned off to the right and onto a proper hiking trail away from the paved park road up a small set of wooden stairs.

The first mile was a steady but manageable incline up to and just beyond the CBT trailhead on the eastern edge of Vogel. We crossed over a few small streams on a few small wooden footbridges, passed a small waterfall and eventually came to our first road crossing an hour or so into the day.

The road here was an unpaved gravel forest service road. A sprawling remote campsite was nearby, and a few cars were stationed at a makeshift parking lot near the wooden footbridge we had just traversed. After stopping for a few moments to take in the scene and rest our legs, we continued.

Our hike that morning was mostly uneventful. We talked, made jokes and corralled the dogs while we walked along an even path through the forest. Though we were steadily gaining elevation throughout the morning, the trail beneath our feet was not steep or particularly difficult.

"I feel a lot better than I did in the Smokies," I told Jeremy. "It's almost like carrying less weight actually makes backpacking easier."

"Who would have thought?" he responded.

Jeremy and I shared a similar, mostly vulgar sense of humor. We would need to be on our best behavior this weekend while Lucy was around. Our jokes and banter would mostly consist of innuendo and wordplay.

It never poured, but a light sprinkling persisted throughout the morning. We marched through a brown and grey tunnel under the old forest, passing by backcountry campsites every mile or so until we finally reached the dreaded four-mile climb that would take us up to the Duncan Ridge Trail intersection that was followed by a short half mile or so trek to the Coosa Bald summit.

The grade here was not easy, but it could have been much worse. The trail was free from large rocks, stones and roots to slow our pace. There were no steps, just a steady march upward.

We stopped every so often to rest and grab a drink of water or light snack. Lucy, who had been upbeat earlier in the day, began to slow considerably as we climbed toward Coosa. I began to wonder if she questioned her decision to stuff a few extras in her pack and offered to lighten her pack load.

A little after one in the afternoon, we stopped to eat lunch at a trailside campsite near a small mountain stream. Removing our packs and finding a place to sit for a few moments was a welcome change to the constant inclines we were experiencing. While we snacked, a handful of trail runners silently trotted past us in a single file line. We saw several trail runners throughout the morning. It was difficult to differentiate between the groups. Raven and Prince barked as the group moved quickly away from us up the trail.

After eating and filtering a bit of water, we put our backs on and continued the last few miles toward Coosa, determined to end the day with a fire and a warm meal. The drizzle dampened our surroundings and the overall mood, but the payoff promised to be worth the effort.

I was excited to be on the trail and to spend the night in the forest, but I was ready to be dry, warm and out of the rain for a while.

Lucy, by this point in the afternoon, had all but given up. Jeremy and I offered words of encouragement to help nudge her along, but we were stopping frequently to wait for Lucy to muster the motivation to continue.

"I know it's tough," I told her during a particularly difficult section of trail. "Even if you only put one foot in front of the other or it takes you ten minutes to hike a few feet, you have to keep moving forward. We're almost there, and when we get there, we're going to set up camp and have some tasty food!"

Lucy did not appear visibly fatigued, and I thought her pace might have been as much a product of boredom as tired legs. Still, she perked up as we continued and eventually fell back into a steady rhythm.

Spurred on by the prospect of a warm meal and a chance for an extended rest, we made our way toward the campsite. My legs had grown tired, as well, but I stayed just behind Lucy as we made our way to the top of Coosa.

The last stretch of trail was intense, even for Jeremy and me. For a mile or more there were no breaks for our legs, no chance to walk along an easy, flattened path. The trail climbed higher and higher until we reached the clouds themselves. The ground beneath our feet was now mostly comprised of loose gravel stones and larger rocks. The higher we climbed, the fewer roots we saw as the trees gave way to the mountaintop elevation.

Eventually, the wind began to whip across our faces as a cold and constant breeze. It was then I knew we were close to our highest elevation of the day. We continued up the trail through low-hanging clouds that blanketed the ridgeline, covering the top of the mountain and the trail itself in a thick, soupy fog. It was an incredible sight to behold, both haunting and marvelous.

Around four that afternoon, we arrived at Coosa after passing two campers with their dog just before the Duncan Ridge Trail. The pair, a younger couple, was struggling to maintain a fire while the light rain fell around them. Near their dome tent was a tarp tied to a small tree protecting a collection of twigs, sticks and branches, protecting their fuel from the ongoing rain.

We exchanged hellos but quickly moved off toward Coosa in search of our camp spot. All of us were ready to find a spot to set up for the night, eat and rest.

I was worried that we would encounter another backpacker or group of campers at our planned stop atop the mountain, but as we made our way to the site, it became obvious that we were the only ones on Coosa, save for the couple and their dog that was several hundred yards back down the trail.

After summiting the mountain and finding the elevation marker, we continued down the trail for a short while until we found a suitable spot next to an old, but well-utilized fire ring. The clouds here hovered over the mountain, shrouding the nearby trees and boulders in a deep and damp mist. Massive boulders topped the mountain and the exposed rock under our feet was a reminder of the millions of years of erosion and weather that came long before us.

"Do you think you can get a fire going?" Jeremy asked after we removed our packs and surveyed the site. Water drops from the trees above smacked against the top of my rain jacket's hood while I scanned the nearby fallen limbs and sticks. A pile of wood was gathered next to the stone fire pit leaning against a tree. There were more than enough fallen sticks and branches to make a blazing fire if the conditions were better.

Everything on top of the mountain was wet, including us.

It was no use. All the nearby wood was soaked and the nonstop rains meant that sustaining a fire would be incredibly difficult. On most trips like this, I would have brought some sort of tinder along with me, whether homemade char cloth or some other fire aid. If it was a little drier, I might have been able to make something from what we had available to us.

"Oh, man. I don't think so. Everything is soaked," I told him.

Jeremy was disappointed. For most of the day, our conversations revolved around sitting by a campfire, warming ourselves and enjoying camp foods. Jeremy had brought along a small bottle of bourbon, and there was a miniature box of wine in my pack, as well.

The top of the mountain was much colder than the valley below thanks to the wind. We had climbed more than 2,000 feet since the morning, and the temperature dropped substantially the higher we climbed.

The sun was making its way toward the horizon and had difficulty cutting through the dense fog and clouds hanging all around us.

It was cold. We were cold. And the sun would soon be gone, making the mountaintop even colder. A fire would have made for a better ending to the day.

Our first task was to set up camp. Lucy and I found a soft spot for the tent several yards off the trail and went about setting up our temporary shelter. After the tent was constructed, I went about preparing dinner while the light rain continued down on us from above.

I pulled out the small propane stove from my pack and set to boiling a pot of water for Lucy's dehydrated meal. Water was scarce during the second half of the day, but we felt like we had enough to make it through to the next morning. I did worry that if we didn't collect and filter water soon after departing camp, we would be thirsty to start our second day.

Lucy ate a chili mac dehydrated meal, while I set to boiling a small pot for my own dinner. I ate chicken and rice while Raven scarfed a cup of dog food. Jeremy made his own chili mac and ate a cup of ramen.

After eating and hanging our food and trash bags, we decided to lay down in our tents. Without a fire, and with the steady dripping of water down on our heads from the leaves above, sitting outside in the hazy cold was unappealing.

As we approached our tent, I noticed that Lucy had left the tent door open before we ate dinner, and a fair amount of water had dripped into the tent through the door while we ate. I used a spare shirt to wipe away as much water as I could before we laid down, but the dampness lingered on our sleeping bags and the tent floor.

I was too exhausted to be upset, but the damp sleeping bag would make it difficult to get warm.

Raven slept next to Jeremy's tent to be near Prince, who we jokingly referred to as her boyfriend, while Lucy and I crawled into my single-person tent. It was cramped, wet and cold, but before too long, we eventually warmed up in our sleeping bags. The ground beneath us was soft and free from loose rocks and sticks. The drops of water against the tent's roof provided an inconsistent but pleasant natural rhythm to the night.

Lucy changed into pajamas and crawled into her sleeping bag, shivering. We cuddled together for warmth while Raven wandered back and forth between our tent and Jeremy's, occasionally crashing into his tent wall in an effort to get inside.

I put Tim Burton's "The Corpse Bride" on my phone for us to watch until we fell asleep.

***

It was freezing. The night had been brutally cold, and both Lucy and I woke up several times overnight for several reasons: soreness, cold or hearing Raven's rustling outside. The patch of ground where I had set up the tent was soft, but sleeping on the ground was still, well, sleeping on the ground. I missed sleeping in a hammock.

"Dad, I have to pee," Lucy told me as she stirred in her sleeping bag long before the sun had risen.

It wasn't even six in the morning, and the idea of leaving the tent to escort Lucy to a secluded spot in the woods was not how I wanted to begin my day. After a bit of coaxing, and the threat of her ruining her new sleeping bag, I dressed, put on my boots and ventured out into the cold to help Lucy find a spot to relieve herself. Raven ran over to greet us as we climbed out of the tent.

The entire mountaintop was shrouded in a grey haze from the clouds that had settled during the previous night. It was as if we were camping in Stephen King's "The Mist." The views here may have been incredible on a cloudless day, but the mist offered an equally interesting vantage. I took a few photos of our surroundings, as I had never camped in a setting like this before. Our visibility might have been 20 feet in any given direction.

Lucy walked off to find a spot to use the restroom while I fed Raven and gave her water. A few moments later, I heard a group of trail runners quickly approaching our camp from the top of Coosa. They must have had an incredibly early start to the day to make it to Coosa's summit before the sun appeared.

Raven ran over to meet them and jump on and greet each one individually. There were two women and one man in the group. They didn't seem too bothered by Raven's uninvited introductions, but it was still embarrassing to not have control over my dog's behavior.

"Oh, geez, I'm so sorry," I told them as I pulled Raven away. "We're probably ruining your times." We exchanged a few awkward laughs, and the trio quickly went on their way. I held onto Raven for a few seconds until the trail runners were out of sight, but as soon as I left her go, she sprinted full speed down the mountain to chase after them.

"Raven!" I shouted as loud as I could, but it was no use. She had disappeared into the mist without a moment's hesitation.

"Grab Raven's leash," I shouted to Lucy as I took off as fast as I could down the mountain. It was more than a hundred yards of running full sprint before I caught the group, who had stopped and were now more than politely annoyed with my dog.

"Sorry, so sorry," I apologized between gasps of air. "I didn't realize I'd be doing any trail running today, too."

The joke helped soften the glare I was receiving from the man in the group. He was short, and thin, with a lengthy beard that dropped well below his chin. He scoffed and turned around to continue the morning run.

I grabbed Raven by the collar and walked her slowly back up the mountain, painfully gasping for air as the trail runners continued. We eventually ran into Lucy who was coming down the trail to meet us, and I attached Raven's leash as we made our way back to camp.

Once there, I tied Raven to a tree and laid back down in the tent, too exhausted and out of breath to feel the cold. Raven whined for the next hour while Lucy and I attempted to nap away the morning cold.

Soon after, the frigid temperatures became too much to bear. I got out of the tent again, hoping that moving around would help us stay warm. Jeremy stirred and got up a few minutes later, while Lucy and I went to collect the food bags so we could prepare breakfast.

I packed away the tent, stuffing the contents into my pack's outside pocket to keep the wet tarp away from the still-dry contents inside my bag. The rain stayed away that morning, but the lingering mist ensured everything remained damp.

After I finished breaking down our gear, I boiled the last bit of water from my bottle to make our dehydrated breakfasts; biscuits and gravy.

I still carried about a liter of water in my bladder, tucked comfortably in my pack, but given the choice between bladder water and water from a bottle, I have always chosen water from a bottle.

The biscuits and gravy went a long way toward warming our bodies and lifting our spirits. Lucy was especially fond of the meal and later commented that it had been her favorite part of the entire trip. It might have been mine, as well. Holding the bags warmed our hands, and once inside our bellies, we felt ready to come down the mountain.

After breakfast, we set off from the top of Coosa down the Duncan Ridge Trail back toward the CBT intersection. I've always preferred starting the mornings on relatively flat and easy trails to help slowly acclimate my legs and lungs to the miles ahead. Thankfully, this section of trail was an uncomplicated way to start the morning.

Around a mile into the day, the trail became steep and rocky as the path continued down the mountain. We slowly made our way down the rocky slope, carefully watching our feet and urging the dogs to slow their pace until we reached the safer footing. We left the clouds behind as we walked further down the mountain, escaping the mist and fog above. Another flat section followed, and we approached Wolf Pen Gap Road, the first paved road crossing from the north around 11 that morning.

The familiar sounds of motorcycles filled the air from the valley below. North Georgia, especially this area of the Blue Ridge Mountains, is a popular destination for motorcycle riders who flock here to tackle the winding bends. The distinct sound of Harley Davidsons, street and adventure bikes nudged us, albeit briefly, back to the reality of the modern world.

A short while later, the road came into full view below. A few hundred yards before the trail crossed over the pavement, we saw something wholly unexpected.

"Trail magic!"

Three milk jugs filled with untreated water sat under a blazed tree. Jeremy was ecstatic, as he had been running low with only about a half liter of water left in his water bag, and the next water source was still a few miles away according to our map. Water sources were scarce on this side of the loop, and it would be a few miles before we came across a suitable stream to refill our bottles.

It might not have been a cache of candy bars or someone giving out grilled hot dogs by the road, but the sight of the water lifted our spirits. Someone, somewhere provided for us. We were grateful for the gesture.

Our group stopped to rest and watched the passing motorcycles while Jeremy collected water. One of the jugs advised backpackers to filter before consuming, which was no problem for Jeremy as his pack's bladder system included a built-in filter.

"That's the first time I've ever seen trail magic," I told Jeremy. "This is awesome."

"Me too," Jeremy responded as he poured a bit of the water into Prince's lapping mouth.

"What's trail magic?" Lucy inquired.

"Well, it's when people give away things to hikers, like food and water and candy bars and stuff," Jeremy responded. "Sometimes people set up their cars along the trail and give or sell things to hikers like us for cheap just to be nice."

Trail magic is far more common on the Appalachian Trail or other long-distance backpacking trails than on loops like the one here near Vogel. Perhaps our proximity to the AT itself was the reason why someone chose this spot to leave this mark of kindness.

We made our way to Wolf Pen Gap Road and spotted the familiar lime green blaze of the CBT on the other side of the paved mountain road. The trail here was now climbing up to Slaughter Mountain, another one of Georgia's highest peaks. Thankfully, the path seemed to skirt around the direct summit, which meant we wouldn't have to ascend the entire 4,337 feet, but we would come close during the ascent.

The trail was incredibly steep from the road. Lucy stopped every 20 feet or so to rest for a moment, but she was never out of breath. Jeremy and I, however, old and slow, huffed and puffed the entire trek to the top of Slaughter, moaning and continuously begrudging the incline.

In this section, it wasn't my legs that suffered, it was my lungs. I was sympathetic to Lucy's pace and did my best to encourage her to continue without stopping as often. But in truth, I was thankful that she was stopping as often as she was since it allowed me the opportunity to catch my breath, as well.

"Slow and steady wins the race," I told her.

We crossed the paved road below around noon and were still climbing up to the top of the ridge an hour later when we stopped long enough to remove our packs and sit down. I laid down on a bed of leaves beside the trail, ignoring the rocks, sticks and other debris on the ground beneath my back. It felt good to rest for more than a few minutes.

Lucy and I have typically hiked between eight and ten miles during an average day hike. And while some backpackers or day hikers could undoubtedly tackle the entire 13 miles of the CBT in one day, we struggled on the steep uphill portions of the trail during the second day. Even with a lighter pack and an entire day ahead of me, I didn't know that I would have been able to make the entire loop in a single day. The terrain here was as difficult as any I experienced on the AT.

"Do you know what hikers talk about when they're on the trail?" I asked Lucy to keep her mind off of her legs and the incline still ahead of us.

"What?" she responded.

"Food!" Jeremy exclaimed from up the trail.

"That's right! What do you want to eat for dinner? I want a chicken fried steak, some mashed potatoes and gravy, cream corn, two pieces of cornbread..." I said, trailing off into an endless stream of traditional southern foods.

"I want all of that, too," Lucy said.

"I want fried chicken!" Jeremy responded.

"I want that, too!" Lucy said.

We continued the talk about food and our plans for dinner that evening as we left our resting spot.

A dozen or more short rest breaks later, we finally arrived at the ridgeline and the highest elevation of the day, signaling the end of our last daunting uphill portion. The hike from then on was much easier on the lungs and the legs. We continued until we found a campsite near the intersection of the Blood Mountain approach trail to the AT and CBT. It was around two in the afternoon and we stopped to eat lunch. This campsite was likely the closest site in the area to the AT and Blood Mountain, another one of Georgia's highest peaks.

Lucy ate a chocolate bar, a few meat sticks and a granola bar. I had beef jerky, peanuts and a chocolate bar. Jeremy opened a pack of flavored tuna that didn't appear to me to be particularly appetizing, but he didn't seem to mind.

The three of us shared a pack of M&Ms.

We relaxed in the afternoon sun, enjoying a few moments of walking around without the weight of our packs pulling us down. The campsite was massive and featured an impressive fire pit complete with benches made from the logs of fallen trees and several nearby rocks. Many people must have put in quite a bit of effort to craft this spot into such a picturesque campsite. A half dozen or more tents could have been comfortably arranged here.

Coosa Bald was still visible through the forest, as was Slaughter Mountain where we had just descended.

Another trail runner, this time a man with a majestic, almost dwarven beard and small frame, waved as he passed us, before quickly fading off into the distance.

Soon, it was time to set off again. The last mile or two of the loop seemed to go on forever, as they always do on these kinds of hikes. There was still nearly a thousand feet to descend, and the rocky trail beneath our feet was unforgiving after the weekend mileage we had put in. The soft trail we had recently experienced gave way to more gravel and loose stones, challenging our footing and pace. Both Prince and Raven pulled ahead on the descents while trying to avoid the smaller stones.

After a short while, we made our way to a mountain stream featuring a series of short, but scenic, waterfalls that fed into a larger stream in the valley below. We pushed on until we spotted one of Vogel's pioneer camping shelters down the hill to our right. The sight inspired us to finish the day as we finally reentered Vogel.

"Yep, I'm ready to be done," I told Jeremy and Lucy several times late that afternoon. My legs were sore and my feet were tender from the rocks and roots we traversed over the last few miles. My shoulder ached from my pack weight, and my stomach was ready for a full meal.

"Me too," Lucy responded.

We were all exhausted by this point. Jeremy and I limped down the trail attempting to avoid the loose rocks and roots beneath our feet. Jeremy lost his footing a few times on the loose stones and cringed briefly with pain and worry, but he never seriously injured himself. This section, at the end of our hike, proved to be one of the most difficult sections of the weekend. Fatigue began to creep over our group. We were distracted by our tired legs and empty bellies.

Lucy was more upbeat on the downhill portion, stopping far less frequently than she had earlier in the day during the ascent up to Slaughter Mountain. This made our expected arrival time far more reasonable than it would have been if we had continued at our early afternoon pace.

Around four, we finally made it back to the trailhead sign we had first spotted more than 24 hours before. Lucy walked Raven as we pressed toward the Vogel visitor center and back to civilization. Backcountry campsites came into view on the right, and a few moments later, the paved road appeared below us.

The smell of campfires and grilled hot dogs permeated the air. We stopped for a moment on an overlook while Jeremy took a photo of the three of us to commemorate the successful weekend adventure. Despite snacking less than two hours earlier, all three of us were solely focused on our next meal.

"Run ahead down the stairs so you can be the first one done," I told Lucy after Jeremy snapped a few photos of the three of us.

She ran ahead and climbed down the stairs, waiting for the rest of our group to finish. A few seconds later, I came down the stairs, officially ending the hike.

"You were the first one done," I exclaimed. "Congrats!" Jeremy and I both offered Lucy a celebratory high-five.

I had tried to be as encouraging as possible during the hike, our most difficult so far. The tough moments, like the final mile or two of our climb up to Coosa Bald or the ascent up to Slaughter Mountain, had been difficult for her, but Lucy pulled through. We all pulled through together. I was proud and hoped that I conveyed that sense of pride to her.

I was also impressed with how Jeremy interacted with Lucy. For a man in his 40s with no children of his own, he had been as calm and encouraging as any father I've ever met. A lesser man might have been flustered or frustrated during our many breaks, but he had been kind throughout our two days on the trail.

We made it back to the car a little after five that afternoon. I went to the visitor center to buy a park sticker and present for Lucy, hoping a prize would help cement the positive experience in her mind. I loaded the packs onto the Jeep's roof rack while Jeremy and Lucy ran off to the restrooms.

In total, we had hiked more than 16 miles over the two days, climbing and descending more than 5,000 feet over two of Georgia's highest mountains. My legs felt stiff and my feet could have been pancakes. But my spirits were surprisingly high.

After we loaded our gear onto the roof rack and piled into the car and set off, our attention turned to dinner. We stopped at Big D's bar-b-que in Dawsonville, a now-favorite spot on the way home from our north Georgia adventures.

Jeremy and I ate ribs and wings while Lucy had a hotdog and fries (and a few of my wings). It might not have been that chicken fried steak I had so badly craved while on the trail, but the meal was just what I needed.

We laughed at our sore bodies as we hobbled from the ordering line to our table. We shared our favorite moments from the trail as we enjoyed dinner until it was finally time to return to the real world.

Bartram Trail & Chattooga River Trail

THREE DAYS. TWO NIGHTS. 40 MILES.

This was the Georgia section of the Bartram Trail through the Chattahoochee National Forest in Rabun County.

While not as well-known as some of the other trail networks in Georgia, like the Appalachian Trail or the Benton MacKaye Trail, the BT offers backpackers and day hikers a variety of sights and scenes as it meanders through the north Georgia wilderness and should be considered among the state's best long distance backpacking offerings.

The BT is named after famed naturalist and author William Bartram, a true explorer in a time when exploration and wild adventure was still possible in the American Southeast. Though many of the lands he visited were long settled and cultivated by Native Americans before his day, Bartram was one of the first European descended explorers of the area, outside of a handful of traders and early trappers, to experience much of Appalachia's secluded beauty. Before Bartram, no one so carefully documented the geography, plants and animals of the region.

Bartram, whose father was appointed by King George III as a royal botanist and charged with exploring and cataloging English territory in the New World, also took up the mantle as an explorer after successful excursions during his youth. The BT follows as closely to Bartram's paths as possible thanks to references, intricate notes and detailed maps that he included in his writings.

For more than four years, Bartram's travels took him across North Carolina, South Carolina, Georgia, Alabama and Florida, where he notated fauna and flora, met with native tribes and explored some of the region's most impressive natural sites.

While his contributions to American natural history are known to some, Bartram's writings, drawings, catalogs and overall influence are not widespread outside of historical and naturalist circles. This naturalist, unfortunately, has faded into relative obscurity over time while others, like Charles Darwin and Henry David Thoreau, have lingered in the spotlight of popular culture.

Bartram wrote extensively about the natural history of the region and was most famous for his book "Travels through North and South Carolina, Georgia, East and West Florida, the Cherokee Country, etc.

His book made him a minor celebrity in his own time, and by all accounts, he lived a comfortable life after returning to his home in Kingsessing, Pennsylvania, where he worked alongside his brother overseeing and expanding upon his father's botanical garden, until his death in 1823.

Bartram's Garden still exists to this day and is the oldest botanical garden in North America.

Bartram's explorations and catalogs of wildlife and plant life may only be overshadowed by his accounts of his interactions with early traders, settlers and Native Americans, particularly those of the Cherokee Nation.

In his book "Travels," Bartram wrote at length about the already-strained relationship between the Cherokee, and other native tribes, and the European settlers moving into the American Southeast to stake a claim to the land and resources.

One such description included in his work centers around a haunting retelling of the aftermath of a battle between Cherokee warriors and settlers from Carolina that ended in a disastrous defeat for the natives.

"At this place was fought a bloody and decisive battle between the Indians and the Carolinians, under the conduct of general Middleton, when a great number of Cherokee warriors were slain, which shook their power, terrified and humbled them, insomuch that they deserted most of their settlements in the low countries, and betook themselves to the mountains as less accessible to the regular forces of the white people," Bartram detailed.

His writings did not shy away from the reality of the day. Even in the late 1700s, conflicts between Native Americans and European settlers were commonplace in the Appalachian wilderness as settlers continued their expansion into the native lands, taking whatever resources they could at the expense of the people who inhabited them. Bartram's words foreshadowed the bleak future yet to come for the Cherokee and other native nations of the region.

Despite the mistrust between the colonists and natives, Bartram was often welcomed into Native American villages and wrote fondly of his interactions with the indigenous peoples. His writings included many examples of communing and staying among the Cherokee as an honored guest.

For this trip, I would follow in William Bartram's footsteps from the North Carolina and Georgia border, down into north Georgia and finally ending at the border with South Carolina on the Chattooga River utilizing the aptly named Chattooga River Trail for the final 10 miles back to the car. This adventure, somewhere between 37 and 40 miles in total, would take me over Georgia's second highest peak, Rabun Bald, and offer many miles of ridgeline and riverside backpacking.

I decided to tackle the Bartram Trail for two reasons. The first was that I would be able to complete the entire 40-mile section in three days of hiking. The second reason was the fact that many of the local hotspots, particularly those on the AT or BMT, would be over-crowded due to the recent start of the spring thru-hike season. Space and privacy on any of the AT trails or even some of the nearby trail networks would be scarce.

The AT has surged in popularity in the last two decades. Seeking isolation on the world's most popular long-distance backpacking trail seemed possible in Georgia only during the fall months.

The hardest day of hiking would undoubtedly be my first on the BT. Rabun Bald, a behemoth by Appalachian standards, was my first and most formidable obstacle. Featuring an old stone fire tower, Rabun Bald is a popular mountain destination for day hikers and backpackers alike.

Since I was hiking the trail north to south, I would begin my trek with Rabun Bald and continue toward the Chattooga.

After reading about the trail and its conditions, I learned that hiking from the north to the south was the most common route chosen by backpackers. While not completely downhill from Rabun onward, the trail south generally trended downward in elevation after summiting Rabun Bald.

In the week prior to the hike, I arranged to shuttle to the North Carolina border trailhead with Chattooga Whitewater Outfitters, a local kayak and rafting shop located just across the state line into South Carolina from Georgia.

The outfitters shop typically deal with those seeking adventure on the water, but they also offer shuttle services to backpackers. This was a blessing, as finding a shuttle service in rural South Carolina proved incredibly difficult in the days leading up to the trip. I had even asked my sister, who lived some two hours away in North Carolina, if she would be able to transport me before finding the outfitters' shuttle service.

"Do you offer shuttle services to backpackers?" I asked Mike, one of Chattooga Whitewater Outfitters' employees over the phone a week before the trip.

"We do," he responded. "Where are you going?"

"I want to do the Bartram Trail, leaving Friday morning up to Rabun Bald and coming back Sunday along the Chattooga River Trail. Are you familiar with the trails?"

"I am, but that's kind of far away. How long are you looking to hike? Maybe we can find you something shorter."

"About 40 miles," I told him.

"Ah. How many people?"

"Just me and my dog."

"Oh, it'll be kind of expensive."

"How much?"

"Like 75 bucks," he said.

"Deal."

An hour in the car and the logistics of the trip made 75 dollars seem like a bargain. When Mike said the trip would be expensive, I had assumed he meant much more than that. I agreed to the offer immediately and emailed him my itinerary a short while later to confirm my plans.

I spent a good deal of time ahead of the trip researching the trail and my planned stops. The Georgia section of the trail was officially marked at 36.5 miles, but spur trails leading to sights along the way like overlooks and waterfalls would put my total mileage well over 40 by the time I reached my car back at the Chattooga River.

Because I was cutting the last 10 miles out of the BT in favor of hiking back toward South Carolina utilizing the Chattooga River Trail over roughly the same amount of distance, I wasn't completely certain of what my actual mileage would be with only a rough estimate to go by.

Still, I knew my calculations couldn't have been that far off.

I pieced together as much information as I could from unofficial maps and other sources I found online, but in truth, my itinerary was not as complete as I would have preferred. A few books on the Bartram Trail were available online, but most of these were printed copies, extra weight I did not want to carry with me on the trail. I opted to make my own guide with maps, an elevation profile and notes instead. I laid out descriptions of the trail and areas of interest on one side of a printed page while the other side had the route and elevation profiles.

Ad hoc trips like this one require careful planning to make the most of the available resources and time, particularly when the adventure is not previously well-documented or a popular destination. Creating my own route from the existing trail network required more consideration than usual.

Resources, like maps, trail descriptions and campsite locations are readily available to section hikers tackling the AT or BMT, but for trips like this, finding comprehensive information can be a bit more difficult. Backcountry campsites are often not well advertised, and other resources, like destinations for springs, are also hit or miss. Backpacking this way requires preparing for the unknown.

I like to think of these trips as a "Choose Your Own Adventure" story.

Three days of hiking meant that my average mileage each day would need to be somewhere in the range of 10 to 15 miles to ensure that I would arrive back at the car in time to head back to Atlanta for work the following Monday. While the distance was not impossible for me on friendly terrain, it would still be the longest stretch of miles that I would complete in such a brief period.

Thankfully, the toughest section of the trail was early on Friday with the climb up to Rabun Bald, and the next two days would largely consist of descents and short elevation gains. The last 10 miles or so, what I had planned for the final day, were very moderate in elevation gain and loss as I would walk along the river.

To help ensure that I could meet my goal, I planned to go as lightweight as possible. I was also prepared to do a bit of night hiking just in case my pace was too slow during the day or the miles too great.

It's often said that backpackers pack their fears. For me, this has always manifested itself as carrying too much food. I've always been afraid of going hungry on the trail or losing my way in the wilderness while hunger and weakness overtook me.

For food, I packed three dinners, all dehydrated Mountain House meals. My personal favorites, chicken and rice, sweet and sour pork and chili mac were included. I also grabbed Pop-Tarts for breakfast, Clif bars for lunch, a pound of peanuts, meat sticks, crackers, cheese, Snickers candy bars and a handful of Girl Scout cookies to include in my food bag. Even with everything I packed, I was still worried about going to sleep hungry every night.

Raven had 10 cups of food, six of which she carried in her backpack that had small plastic containers for water and food. The other four cups, which I considered her emergency stash, were tucked away in my pack for safekeeping.

In the last few days before our planned departure, I packed and repacked my bag several times, checking each time to see if I had forgotten something important or necessary for my survival or comfort. Even with the extensive planning and preparations, I went to sleep the night before the trip feeling as though I was leaving left something crucial out of my pack.

***

My final workday before the trip was uneventful. I answered a few emails, attended a couple of meetings and found that by the middle of the day my thoughts were already drifting to the mountains, far away from my cubicle or responsibilities.

As I packed my car that evening, I held off the urge to immediately drive north, knowing that waiting for traffic to die down from home was a better alternative than sitting in gridlock in an attempt to escape the city early. Once the congestion had died down a bit, I made one last gear check and around 7 p.m. that night Raven and I set off for the family cabin in Long Creek, South Carolina to spend the night ahead of the hike. From there, I would leave the next morning around 7:30 a.m. to ensure that I arrived at the outfitters by my planned shuttle departure time at 8 a.m.

The drive was uneventful. Raven sat in the front passenger's seat as we drove through the darkness to the lone, isolated cabin in the woods of an old country backroad. I listened to Atlanta's NPR station for as long as there was a signal and eventually switched over to a classic rock station when the city fell too far behind me to find on the radio. I stopped for gas in Gainesville and fast food in Clayton.

We arrived at the cabin around two hours after leaving. I laid out my clothes for the morning, crawled into bed and played on my phone for a while before falling asleep just after midnight, anxious for the next morning.

***

It was chilly as I pulled into the parking lot of the Chattooga Whitewater Outfitters shop early Friday morning. An unexpected cold front had moved over the eastern half of the country the week before my trip, dumping snow across much of the northeast and Midwest.

In rural South Carolina, the temperatures were low but expected to rise throughout the weekend, ensuring comfortable middays with chilly nights.

I was the only one in the parking lot as I waited for Mike, my shuttle driver, to arrive. I was somewhat anxious as I ate my breakfast, which consisted of an energy drink and a package of gas station donuts. I'm not often nervous before a hiking trip, but since this hike consisted of just me and Raven for three days, I carried trepidation with me into the start of the first day.

Next to the outfitters was Humble Pie, a local pizza and pasta restaurant only open during the warmer months of the year.

A few minutes before 8 a.m., Mike pulled into the parking lot, waved to me and walked over to open the shop. I finished the world's most unhealthy breakfast and followed him inside to scope out the outfitters.

Despite having land just a few miles down the road and passing the outfitters a hundred times over the last several years, I've never ventured inside Chattooga Whitewater Outfitters.

Several vintage kayaks hung from the ceiling toward the rear of the shop. A series of glass countertops sat in the center of the main room, each containing trinkets like stickers, DVDs and other river-related memorabilia.

Several racks of branded t-shirts and other clothing items were nearby. Supplies, like life vests, rope and other kayak-related gear was also available to purchase or rent.

I introduced myself and walked around the shop while Mike rummaged through the computer and cash register. We chatted while I waited for Mike to finish opening the store.

"You know, my last shuttle driver was named Mike, too," I told him.

"Really? Where was that?"

"A couple of buddies and I did a section of the Smokies last year. Our driver met us at Fontana Dam and took us up to the north end of the park. He was a pretty interesting guy."

"That's funny," Mike said. "It's a pretty common name."

117

"Oh, yeah," I told him. "My dad is named Michael and my first name is Michael, too. I can't escape it!"

I paid Mike for the shuttle and bought a sticker for the Jeep, a somewhat new tradition from adventures I had started in the last year, and prepared to head out.

Mike's son, Eli, was outside with their German Shepherd Zeus wandering the parking lot. As I walked outside, Raven bounced around the front seat of the Jeep, desperately trying to get outside to play with the behemoth of a German Shepard. Zeus was a massive dog, probably three or four times Raven's size and, Mike told me, just over a year old. He was friendly but obviously more interested in playing with Raven than interacting with me.

A few moments later, we set off. I drove the Jeep from the outfitters shop to the bridge at US 76 just a few miles down the road. Mike and Eli followed behind in a small Nissan sedan. The drive to the bridge took just a few minutes. After arriving, I loaded my gear into Mike's trunk, put Raven in the backseat next to Eli and we drove off back toward the outfitters to drop off Eli.

The drive to the trailhead took us up to US 28, the official end of the BT and the border between South Carolina and Georgia. Crossing the bridge here over the Chattooga River into Georgia, we made our way into the Blue Ridge Mountain district of the Chattahoochee National Forest.

Along the way, Mike and I talked about music, his time on the road touring with the Grateful Dead, how long he had worked for Chattooga Whitewater Outfitters, his pizza restaurant and the Chattooga River itself.

"I'm from Augusta," Mike told me as we made our way to the trail.

"Why'd you come up here, the river?"

"Oh yeah," he responded.

I was quickly learning that the Chattooga River was more than a seasonal tourist attraction in the north Georgia mountains. Here, the river was a way of life and supported many of the people in and around Long Creek. The area was a destination for fishing, kayaking, camping and hiking.

The ride to the trailhead was not very long, only around 45 minutes, and the casual conversation helped the time pass.

"You should come by Sunday to eat some pizza at the restaurant," Mike told me as we approached the next turn.

"Definitely. Are you guys open Sunday nights?" I asked.

"We'll be open," he told me. The pizza restaurant was a seasonal affair. During the winter months, when kayaking the Chattooga becomes a bit more difficult thanks to the cold, the restaurant shuts down completely until the following spring. Mike told me that the restaurant was opening this weekend for the first time since the year before.

My plans were set. If I could finish the hike in time, I would destroy a pizza from Humble Pie.

Mike was also organizing a music festival, a three-day event featuring musicians from around the country. This year's festival was its fifth anniversary and was slated to take place at a nearby campground. Most notably, The Marcus King Band was scheduled to headline the Sunday night stage.

"He's like the new Stevie Ray Vaughan," Mike told me excitedly. I promised to listen to his music and even made plans to attend the festival in the summer.

Mike spent a good deal of time in his younger years following the Grateful Dead, but he seemed closer to someone who might have followed Phish instead of the Grateful Dead. He was incredibly enthusiastic about music and was happy to share tidbits about his travels.

Soon, we turned onto an old gravel road, Hale Ridge, and made our way to the trailhead, climbing up the mountains away from the road below. After a few minutes of somewhat carefree mountain driving, Mike pulled over.

"This is you," he said.

I got out of the car, strapped on Raven's pack and then my own. After one final gear check, we were ready to depart. The trailhead climbed immediately from the car and featured a bright lime green trail marker.

I waved goodbye to Mike as Raven and I set off from the trailhead at 9:15 in the morning. The climb up to Rabun Bald, by my estimate, was around two miles with a gain of somewhere around 1,400 feet in elevation. With each step toward the summit, my nervousness began to wear away. My pack fit snugly against my back and shoulders and the conditions on the trail signaled a pleasant day ahead. Raven was attached to a hands-free leash clipped to a nylon belt around my waist.

We marched almost continuously uphill for an hour, stopping every few minutes to rest. As we made our way higher and higher, pockets of snow and ice began to appear on the trail and along the underbrush beside us. The storms from just a few days ago had dumped a few inches of snow on the highest elevations in the area and these had not yet melted. I hadn't expected to see any snow or ice along the trail this late into the year.

Occasionally, a small section of the trail would be completely covered in ice, or a puddle would be frozen, creating an icy crystalline structure made from once watery mud. Initially, I hesitated to step in these sections to preserve the unique formations under my feet but quickly gave up trying to save the muddy ice crystals as my gait and pacing began to suffer as a result. Eventually, I plowed through the frozen puddles with no regard to the natural beauty.

After a while, I checked my map and the elevation profile on my GPS. The elevation gains I expected were not what was under my feet. The trail here was very steep and offered little to no rest on the legs.

The map must be wrong, I thought to myself.

Checking the GPS, I realized that I was several miles southeast of where I should have been. Mike had dropped me off at the wrong approach trail!

121

I was frustrated because this meant I had no knowledge of the trail ahead. My morning route had not been what I expected, and I had no idea how far I was from Rabun Bald, though I was certain that I was still moving toward its summit, as it towered over the other mountains in the area.

The trek seemed to go on forever. After more than two miles of approach trail, I began to wonder if we would make it to the mountaintop by midday.

The forest was still and quiet that morning thanks to the lingering winter. No sounds, human or otherwise, appeared until we nearly reached the summit of Rabun Bald. Off in the distance, I heard several men talking from high above as we approached the old fire tower. The voices gave me hope of a meaningful break, and I pushed on with more fervor than I had in the last two miles.

"We're close," I told Raven as I looked up the mountain through the trees toward the summit. Just up the trail, the fire tower slowly came into view. A few moments later, we reached the peak only a short while after noon.

A group of five or six older men was standing on the old fire tower chatting about the area, the mountain and the local history. Each carried a trekking pole or walking stick, but none carried any substantial weight on their backs. A young couple also walked around the top, snapping photos from their phones and posing against the epic backdrop of the Blue Ridge Mountains behind. Neither of them carried anything on their backs.

I walked over to the wooden stairs, dropped my pack and paused to catch my breath and to take in the 360-degree view offered here.

The final climb to the summit had taken its toll on my body, and my legs and arms, which supported my hiking poles, burned. A rest, even a short one, was necessary.

The wooden stairs were too steep for Raven to climb, so I grabbed her by the handle on her pack and carried her up to the top. When we made it to the wooden platform on top of the stone tower, she eagerly rushed to the group, as far as her leash would allow her. A couple of the day hikers petted her as I surveyed the area. The majesty of the surroundings was breathtaking. Despite a grey backdrop and a limited view of the horizon, I was still able to see many miles off into the distance in every direction I faced.

"Where's Clayton?" I asked one of the hikers.

An older man pointed off to the southwest. "You can see it better on a clearer day," he said. "But, it's down that way a bit." Clayton, the largest nearby city, was 10 or more miles off to the southwest. I looked off and saw a series of roads and buildings in the far distance that I thought resembled the city.

Beegum Gap, a mile or so down the mountain to the north, was the starting point for everyone who came up to the mountaintop that morning. Coming up through Beegum Gap would have been my approach as well, if Mike had not dropped me off at the wrong trailhead. I felt foolish for not questioning where he had dropped me off earlier in the day.

Off in the far distance, two noticeable forest fires burned.

This is why they used to use fire towers, I thought to myself.

I snapped a few photos for a panoramic picture and climbed back down the stairs before the cold, whipping wind made the experience too uncomfortable to bear.

At the base of the tower, I ate my first snack of the day, a Snickers bar with some jerky and cheese.

As I prepared to continue onward to Warwoman Dell, a large group of young, college-aged backpackers came up the mountain. I said hello and introduced myself as Swiss Cheese to the group as they came up the steep hill one-by-one. Ben, Sarah, Zee, Posted and a few other hikers whose names I could not remember approached the tower, dropping their packs for a brief rest and introduced themselves to me.

"Where are you headed?" I asked Ben, the first one up.

"Home now," he responded somewhat relieved. "Where are you from?"

"Roswell, just north of Atlanta," I told him.

"Oh, nice. I live in Gwinnett," he said.

We spoke for a few moments about home, my plans for the weekend and their night in the woods.

"We camped just down the mountain a bit," Ben said. "The stars last night were incredible. Where are you going next?"

"Off to Warwoman, I hope."

"That's 14 miles!"

"Well, I don't know that I'll make it all the way there, but that's right around my midway point, so I'm going to try to get as close as I can to it," I told Ben optimistically.

"Good luck, man!" he said as I strapped into my pack.

Ben and the rest of his group headed up the fire tower as Raven and I made our way toward Warwoman Dell down the BT. This was the first time today that I had actually stepped foot on the BT, and I was anxious to make a good time on the upcoming downhill section.

The voices behind tapered off as we walked under the thick rhododendron covering the trail. The snow and ice gradually disappeared as we made our way further down the mountain, and by mid-afternoon, there were no signs of the recent flurries anywhere.

Around two that afternoon, the sun finally broke through the clouds above, warming the hillside and providing a bit of much-needed energy for the hike. I removed my jacket, placed it in the top pocket of my pack, and soaked up all the warmth my body could handle.

The afternoon hike was largely uneventful. We passed by Wilson Gap and Windy Gap, stopping at the latter for a short rest. While there, a nearby tree fell, spooking both Raven and me, though neither of us saw the tree fall, only hearing the crashing aftermath. The next few miles from Rabun Bald were almost entirely downhill. Raven and I made up a good deal of time on these miles, stopping to rest far less frequently than we had during our ascent up to Rabun earlier that morning.

We continued throughout the late afternoon until dusk, when I began to look for a decent spot to set up camp near a water source. Unfortunately, I was quickly learning that water on the south side of Rabun Bald was difficult to find.

As the sun finally settled behind the nearby hills, we approached Courthouse Gap, just north of Pinnacle Knob, another Appalachian mountain that offered majestic Blue Ridge views. It was here that I decided to make camp for the night, despite the lack of water.

I was disappointed that we had not made it all the way to Warwoman Dell. By my estimate, we were still a few miles to the north. However, after climbing Rabun earlier in the day, and with two days of hiking still ahead of us, I opted to rest and save the strenuous hiking for later in the weekend. I was relieved to know that the hardest part of the hike was well behind us.

I tied Raven to a tree and went about setting up the tent. I removed my sleeping bag, sleeping mat, clothes bag and the electronics from my pack, placing them all inside the tent. The ground here was hard and covered in sticks, loose rock and fallen limbs. I cleared what I could from the ground before popping up the tent, but the darkness made it difficult to find all of the stones and pebbles.

I decided to skip cooking a dehydrated meal and instead ate the last of my day's snacks and hung my food bag on a nearby tree. I also placed my pack off the ground and covered it with its pack cover to protect against the coming rain that was expected the following morning. The weather so far had been grey and cool, but at least the rain had stayed away.

I consulted my map and elevation guide, calculating that we had hiked just over 13 miles that day. The distance was enough to keep us on our planned schedule, and as I crawled into the tent, I took two Ibuprofen pills to help prevent any potential morning soreness. The ground felt as hard as marble, but my sleeping pad made the otherwise miserable surface bearable.

Raven initially hesitated about coming into the tent with me. Even after I had crawled inside, she stood outside the doorway, curiously looking inside. Eventually, after a bit of coaxing, she crawled in and snuggled against my feet, quickly falling asleep.

That night, I watched a few movies on my phone while I tried to rest my legs and body. Eventually, I fell asleep to sounds of sporadic drizzle pattering against the top of my tent and the gentle breeze rustling the trees from above.

***

I woke up Saturday morning around 6 a.m. to the sound of a light breeze and steady rainfall. Poking my head out of the front door of the tent, I saw the grey haze of a cold, foggy morning that enveloped Courthouse Gap while I slept.

I debated whether to get out of my sleeping bag or to wait until the rain stopped to begin the day. Raven was anxious to get outside, but I rolled over and fell back asleep, content to wait out the rain.

Packing up all my gear in the wet was not how I wanted to start the morning.

Nearly two hours later I woke up again, this time intent on breaking camp and hitting the trail, dry or not. Today was my longest planned day, but thanks to the hefty mileage haul the previous day, I was faced with only a 14-mile hike instead of a potential 17-mile trek. The shorter day made sleeping in a bit more tolerable, but I found myself wishing that it had been a clear morning so that I could have gotten an earlier start.

It was already past 8 a.m. I realized there was no more time to delay. With breakfast and packing, I wouldn't be able to hit the trail in less than 30 minutes.

I stumbled out of the tent, fetched my food bag and grabbed Raven's pack that was hanging from a nearby tree. I quickly packed up and prepared to head out after eating a breakfast of crumbled Pop-Tarts and feeding Raven.

The rains had stopped by the time we left camp, though large drops from the tall trees above fell every so often onto the hood of my rain jacket.

We set off from Courthouse Gap around 8:30 that morning, a late start by hiker standards. I had no idea at the time if I would regret the decision to sleep in or if hiking in the rain would ultimately be worth the later arrival to camp that night. The day's elevation profile was not as strenuous as the day before, but I still planned for full day nonetheless.

Although Rabun Bald was far behind us, and we would not come anywhere close to that elevation again over the next two days, there were still plenty of smaller mountains to ascend yet to come.

The trail from camp first led us past Pinnacle Knob, which was accessible from a spur path directly off the Bartram Trail. We continued past the overlook, skirting around the mountain as we climbed throughout the morning. If there had been more time, I likely would have stopped there to check out the views, which I later learned were among the best in the area.

As we moved further away from Rabun Bald, water on the trail became difficult to find. The first major stop along the day's hike was Warwoman Dell, which featured plenty of water and a picnic area where I had initially planned to stop for lunch. Because of the late start, I decided to push my midday meal back to later in the afternoon. I stopped to filter water at Warwoman, however.

The clouds broke around noon, and with the shining sun above us, Raven and I made good time beyond Warwoman Dell. We stopped briefly a few times along the way to check out some of the nearby sites like Becky Branch Falls and Martin Creek Falls but pushed on knowing that any delay would add to our arrival time that night.

By late afternoon, my legs were exhausted. Raven and I rested for a while at Green Gap, a few miles south of Warwoman Dell, while I contemplated the pace that we would need to set to reach camp at a reasonable time that evening. We were over 20 miles into our hike and there was still some eight miles to go before the Chattooga River Trail junction.

Most of the marked mountain gaps on the south side of Rabun

Bald along the trail featured large stone markers, each carefully etched to include the name of the Bartram Trail and the current location. These markers were particularly helpful and each one presented a much-needed morale boost. Some of the markers, like the one I was now sitting on, also displayed the distance to the nearest landmark. In this case, the mark was Warwoman Dell.

It was at Warwoman that I decided to try out a small luxury item I brought with me: a lightweight Bluetooth speaker. I clipped the speaker to my pack and found music from my phone to play.

While we rested, the clouds gathered above and the sky turned a dark grey once again. With the sun now covered, a chill whipped over the ridgeline and throughout the valley. Raven and I set off in an attempt to stay warm and make up some lost time.

A short while later, as we were climbing a particularly challenging hill, I noticed a couple of campers tending to a fire on the top of a nearby ridge. I held Raven close as we approached and turned off the music from my speaker. These were the first people we had seen since leaving Rabun Bald more than a day before, and in her excitement, the little dog pulled me feverishly up the hill to meet her new friends.

The trail here went directly through the center of their camp, and I knew that, if given the chance, Raven would have run amok through the campsite. Two tents were pitched to the right of the site while several hammocks, perhaps three or four, were hanging between handfuls of sturdy pines to the far end of the site.

A man and a woman were walking around the site as Raven and I approached. I waved and said hello from down the hill.

Bob and Jennifer introduced themselves as we passed into their camp. The couple was camping with a Boy Scouts of America expeditionary crew, all of whom were napping or resting in the nearby hammocks.

The last two miles from Green Gap was entirely uphill, so I asked if I could sit down to rest for a while, a request Bob and Jennifer happily obliged.

"Is there any water around here?" I asked the pair as Jennifer pet Raven. I was parched and hopeful for a nearby spring.

"Not up here, but there is some a mile and a half back down the trail," Bob replied. He offered to let me browse through his BT guidebook, but I declined the offer. My trail map and homemade guide said the same about the distance to the next reliable water source, but it was nice to know that there was water coming.

"There is a great campsite less than a mile from here, though," Jennifer chimed in. "No water, but it's gorgeous. Where are you headed?"

"I'm going to the Chattooga River Trail tonight," I told her. "I'm trying to get there by dark."

"You'll really like the Chattooga River Trail," Jennifer said. "We hiked that last year and had a wonderful time."

"How's the trail from here?"

"It's not flat," Bob said. "But, it's a lot easier than what you just came up."

I was relieved. A bit of ridgeline and downhill hiking would be a welcome change from the last few miles. Perhaps I could even make up a bit of time.

A few moments later, after my heart rate had settled and my breathing had returned to normal, Raven and I said our goodbyes and headed down the mountain toward the next gap. The trail ahead followed along the ridgeline for a while, climbing and descending little by little as we made our way ever closer to the river.

The mountains faded into the forest behind us, and though we continued to climb and descend, we were tackling hills now, not mountains. My legs and lungs were grateful for the change of intensity. I again played music as I marched on, singing quietly to myself.

We settled in for the last stretch of trail for the day as dusk transitioned into the night.

We hiked for a long while in the creeping shadows of dusk, but soon the trail became difficult to navigate without additional light. I fumbled in the dark for my headlamp.

The illuminated trail below helped steady my steps, and after a few short breaks, I was relieved to arrive at the trail junction of the Chattooga River Trail and the BT slightly before 8 p.m.

By this point in our hike, my groin had endured enough stress and pressure to ache with each passing step. A slight dull pain accompanied each stride, making for a miserable last mile to the day.

I was thirsty. We hiked several miles since the last water source and my water bottle was empty. Even with the morning rain, the trail was dry and spots along the way where a spring or runoff would have been guaranteed in wetter months were completely devoid of water. My eyes were constantly scanning the nearby forest for any sign of something to alleviate my thirst. Bob and Jennifer's promised water source never materialized, and I felt as though I would have to hike all the way to the Chattooga itself to find something to drink. I knew there would be water sources close to the river.

The BT dumped onto an old forest service road seemingly in the middle of nowhere. A nearby sign showed the BT heading off to the east, while the Chattooga River Trail trailhead was a short walk down the gravel road to the south. We walked through the darkness toward the Chattooga River Trail, hard dirt and rock beneath our feet, until we came across a small clearing near a stream.

This was the spot! I had all but given up hope of finding a comfortable place to sleep that evening and was relieved to finally find a soft grassy patch of land.

A group of campers far off in the distance was having some kind of party or gathering. I could hear drunken screaming and shouting from deep within the woods. They were close but not too close. I couldn't see them, and I knew they couldn't see me through the darkness. It sounded like they were having fun, at least.

The smell of campfire permeated throughout the air and offered a bit of comfort in my otherwise solitary day. Even if I didn't see the campers through the darkness, knowing another group was nearby was still comforting. I hesitated at shouting a greeting back to them through the darkness. In truth, I was too exhausted to muster much of a voice anyway.

I dropped my pack just after 8 p.m. and immediately set out to fill my water bottles. I grabbed two pouches, intent on drinking enough water to make up for the last few parched hours. After filtering the ice-cold water from the stream, I set up the tent and ate the last of the day's snacks. I again opted to skip cooking a dehydrated meal, settling on crackers, meat and cheese, peanuts and whatever else was left over from the day's snack bag. The effort of making a dehydrated meal, plus the time to wait before I could eat it, simply wasn't worth it in my mind. I was too tired to cook and too hungry to wait.

After Raven and I finished chowing down our dinner, I crawled into the tent to lay down. The ground below the tent was soft and covered in grass and fallen leaves, a pleasant change from the previous night's hard dirt and rocky ground.

With Raven curled at my feet, I drifted off to sleep in only a few moments, exhausted from one of my longest ever days of backpacking.

***

The sun was peeking over the nearby hills when I awoke on my last day on the trail.

Today, I would divert away from the BT and continue south toward US 76 on the Chattooga River Trail, bypassing the last 10 miles of the BT off to the north. With the benefit of the morning light, I noticed that we were camped just a few yards away from the actual trailhead where I intended to start our final day on the trail. This was a welcome surprise and meant that my plan to trek out 10 miles was still good to go.

Raven and I had pushed hard the day before, hiking well into the darkness, and our efforts had paid off.

Today was the shortest day by distance and the easiest day of elevation gain and loss for the entire trip. Because we hiked well into the previous night and made up quite a bit of ground lost due to the morning's late start, there were only a handful of miles between us and the Jeep. The distance, early start and refreshed feeling from sleeping on the softer ground raised my spirits quite a bit. I was excited to tackle the day and even more excited about the prospect of a post-hike pizza and beer.

I ate a breakfast of Pop-Tarts and chocolate bars, fed Raven and packed up camp in short order. I was anxious to finish the hike. After checking our GPS location on my phone, I estimated that we could be done by 4 p.m. that afternoon if we left around 9 a.m. that morning, including an hour or so break for lunch. That would put me back home in Atlanta sometime around 8 p.m.

Raven and I set off toward the trailhead, turning left toward the Chattooga River from our campsite by the small forest stream where we had camped the night before. The trail slowly climbed and descended as it meandered its way to the river below. The Chattooga River Trail featured lime green trail markers, much like the Rabun Bald approach trail we completed two days earlier.

After a mile and a half of spirited walking, we came to the trail junction of the Chattooga River Trail and the BT. I turned what I thought was south here and found myself hiking beside a small, bubbly stream. Raven climbed down the nearest embankment and drank a bit of water. We had made excellent time up to this point in the morning.

After a few hundred yards on the Chattooga River Trail, the stream began to move more rapidly and eventually fell over a nearby cliff, dumping out into the Chattooga in an impressive display. Raven and I continued to follow the trail down further before we ran into a severe problem: there was no more trail to follow.

Had I missed another junction somewhere?

Standing on a sandy beach next to the mighty river, I looked up the hills and across the river for a sign, any sign, of the lime green blaze marker indicating where I might have lost the trail. A recent trip along the Jacks River Trail had seen a similar predicament. Thanks to its incredible width (and probably depth), the river here was impassable without a raft or canoe, even in the best conditions.

I walked back up toward the falls and ran into a man, his wife and teenage daughter. All three had come out for the morning to check out the falls and experience a bit of nature for themselves. I asked if they knew which trail we were on.

"This is the Dick's Creek Falls trail," the man told me.

I was floored. This was nowhere close to where I needed to be by this point in the day. Dick's Creek Falls was nowhere on my itinerary. I had not seen it on the map that morning while planning the day's route. I had no idea where I was, only where I had come from.

I pulled out my phone and looked at the GPS data. True enough, I had walked more than two miles in the wrong direction, downhill nearly the entire way. I hung my head in shame as I slowly made my way back up the hills toward the spot we had camped the night before.

Not only had I added nearly four miles to my trip total, I had also given myself at least two more hours for the day. My goal of finishing the day by mid-afternoon was crushed. It was now looking more like an early evening finish instead of a late afternoon finish.

The walk back to the trailhead was slow and arduous. The trail here, though not steep, inclined upward much of the way back to our previous night's camp. My spirits were low from the mistake in direction, which also sapped much of my energy and slowed my stride. After more than an hour of hiking at a snail's pace, we arrived back to the first junction we turned at earlier in the day.

Back at the trailhead I sat on a fallen tree and ate a late-morning snack. It was nearly noon, and both Raven and I were already tired from the push back uphill toward the previous night's camp. After filtering a bit of water, we set off again, this time in the right direction.

The trail climbed here and moved away from the Chattooga River. We marched onward and upward for a few miles until we came back down to the river for a lengthy stretch of riverside hiking.

The sandy path beneath my feet felt refreshing, and I pushed hard in this section to make up for any lost time on the uphill and forced backtracking from earlier in the day.

After a while, the trail again moved away from the river and back into the rolling hills above. Each summit was less strenuous than the one before, and eventually, there were no more mountains to climb as we approached the last stretch of trail back to US 76 and to the car.

The afternoon seemed to drag on forever. The trail ahead of me was seemingly never-ending. Bends and switchbacks along the trail were common here but each eventually blended together in a blur of forest green and brown.

Raven and I rested often that afternoon. My stomach ached from hunger and my thirst seemed unquenchable. I drank more than four liters of water in those last 10 miles, stopping at every opportunity to filter stream water to fill my bottles. After the previous day's overall lack of water, I made sure to take every chance to hydrate.

Hiking became difficult later in the afternoon as my legs grew tired from the weight of my pack, the extra miles and the rocky path and my once again aching groin. As is often typical of these trips, I packed too much food, and my bag weighed several more pounds than it should have if I ate all that I brought with me.

We were still several miles from the Jeep by 4 p.m., which had been my original goal. I was ready to be done. I recommitted to finishing by 6 p.m. and decided to take fewer breaks for the rest of the afternoon.

Raven and I pushed hard throughout the last stretch of trail to finish before the sun fell.

I saw no one in the forest that day outside of a mountain biker who had quickly passed us early in the morning and the family at Dick's Creek Falls who so graciously pointed out our directional dysfunction.

The day, much like the previous two, was a lonely, solitary experience for Raven and me. She didn't seem to mind the isolation, however, and was eager to tackle whatever miles were left ahead of her, even when I forced us to stop and rest for a few moments.

Toward the end of the day, Raven would close her eyes and catch a quick nap whenever we stopped for more than a few minutes. Regardless, once it was time to again move, she popped up and wagged her tail to let me know she was ready to go.

Is it still a cat nap if it's performed by a dog?

The trail followed high above the Chattooga for much of the afternoon, but the river was barely visible from our vantage point through the trees leading down into the valley.

The penultimate mile of the trail saw the Chattooga peek through the trees off to our left. Sounds and sights of families playing and exploring the river below began to fill the forest as we pressed on toward our destination. It was a warm, sunny afternoon and even as the late afternoon approached, the sun continued to shine brightly through the leaves above us.

The river came into full view as the trees disappeared from the hill below and the bridge over US 76, our last official hurdle, was first spotted just after 5:30 that evening. I welcomed the sound of cars, as it signaled the end of a long and exhausting three days.

Raven and I made it to the bridge just after 6 p.m. that evening. The last marker, a board with bear notices, a rough trail map and other Chattahoochee National Forest information, signaled the official end of the hike.

The last stretch of trail on a lengthy backpacking trip always feels like the longest. I've written about this before, but the last mile is always the longest. Perhaps it's exhaustion or some sort of mental block that drags out the day. Or perhaps there's a phenomenon that bends and stretches time and space which only affects hikers.

Finally, the trail dumped out beside the road and crossed over the Chattooga River on an impressively wide concrete two-lane bridge. We climbed the final staircase and reached the Jeep back at the parking lot, some 43 miles from where we had started just over two days before.

Dropping my pack beside the car, I sat on the hard concrete for a few moments, drinking the last bit of water I had filtered earlier in the day. Raven collapsed beside me, quickly closing her eyes.

Knowing that I was free from the risk of running out of food and water was immensely liberating. After packing my gear into the back of the Jeep, I rested a few more moments before finally loading into the car.

In total, we hiked over 14 miles that day, four more than originally planned thanks to the unexpected visit to Dick's Creek Falls that morning. Over the three days, we walked more than 40 miles altogether, right in line with how far I expected to hike.

The trip was physically demanding in a way that I hadn't experienced since my Appalachian Trail section hike through the Great Smoky Mountains National Park a year earlier. That trip featured shorter days, on average, but the elevation gains and losses were far more strenuous. Outside of Rabun Bald, none of the mountains I had crossed were anywhere close to those commonly found in the Smokies. Still, the Bartram Trail offered a demanding challenge.

I loaded my pack and poles into the car. Raven collapsed in the passenger's seat as I took my place behind the wheel. I turned on the car and blasted the air conditioning while finishing the last bit of my water.

"Food!" I shouted to myself, startling Raven.

It was time to feast. I drove off in search of that Humble Pie pizza and a beer or two to celebrate.

The Foothills Trail & King Creek Falls Trail

OUTSIDE OF THE WORLD FAMOUS Appalachian Trail and the not-quite-as-famous Benton MacKaye Trail, the Foothills Trail, which straddles the state line between South Carolina and North Carolina for 77 miles, is perhaps the region's most well-known and physically challenging backpacking experience.

The Foothills Trail runs from Oconee State Park to Table Rock State Park, both located in upstate South Carolina. Thanks to a generous donation from Duke Energy, operators of coal and nuclear power plants in the region, the trail moved from a pipedream to a reality more than 30 years ago during the height of the late 20th-century environmental movement.

Many organizations invested in the trail's early development. The United States Forest Service, South Carolina Department of Parks, Recreation and Tourism, Pendleton Historic and Recreational Commission, Duke Power and Clemson University's Recreation and Park Administration Department all collaborated to plan for and begin work on the Foothills Trail.

The FT initially began as a loose connection of trails in and around the two South Carolina state parks with the goal of eventually connecting Oconee and Table Rock via a unified trail network. After more than a decade of hard work by volunteers, the trail officially opened in 1981.

Much like Georgia's Vogel State Park, Oconee and Table Rock were both products of the New Deal-era Civilian Conservation Corps (CCC) program. Work began on both parks during the 1930s which included constructing many of the trails and park facilities that are still in use almost 100 years later.

The FT had been on my radar for a while.

After watching a few videos of trail experiences online and reading about the trail in detail during the preceding months, I set my mind to completing the FT in mid-spring. Having recently backpacked the Bartram Trail, which challenged my physicality and pushed me harder than I had expected, I was more cautious than usual while planning for the FT.

I was familiar with the conditions of the trail and what to expect after hiking to White Water Falls the previous year with Lucy. At 411 feet, the upper falls, located in North Carolina's Nantahala National Forest, is among the tallest waterfalls in the Eastern United States. The lower falls, some two miles downriver in Sumter National Forest, while not as towering as the upper falls, is still impressive at over 200 feet tall.

The route we took to visit the falls was a short spur trail that connected with the FT at the Whitewater River. The massive rock outcrops here are stunning, and the river is wild thanks to the falls high above. After experiencing just a few brief miles of the trail, I was hooked.

A few weeks ahead of my planned thru hike of the FT, I began gathering supplies, organizing my trip and mentally preparing for the trek.

Weight, as always, was a concern for me as I packed away meals and snacks for the trip. Following my recent hike of the BT and the difficulty finding reliable water, I was prepared to make do with less, carry more water between sources and to refill my bottles completely at every opportunity. Thankfully, the FT featured plentiful water sources as it followed closely along several rivers and hugged Lake Jocassee for many miles.

My backpack was filled with much of the same gear I carried with me on the Bartram Trail a month or so earlier. I had treated the BT as a trial run for the Foothills Trail and was ultimately pleased with my gear choices and how it performed in the real world.

I again carried my single person Alps Mountaineering Zephyr 1 tent, opting to sleep on the ground instead of in a hammock. I managed to cut a bit of additional weight by removing a handful of smaller items that had either failed on the BT or that were never once used.

Every time I wrap up a backpacking trip, while unpacking my bag, I find myself removing some piece of gear that I never used. It takes time to learn exactly what is and is not required on a trip, and each trip is different. Every backpacker has his or her own set of must-have gear. Shelter, water and food are essential. What kind of shelter, how much food and how you obtain water is always up for debate and personal preference.

It's too easy to grab more and more things, stuffing them into your pack until it bulges with excess weight, stealing valuable space. Long distance backpackers often preach weight reduction. Is that heavy pocket knife worth the added weight if a small utility blade can do the job just as well? Do you really need to carry a pair of socks for each day on the trail? Why carry a full-length toothbrush when you can saw off most of the handle?

Some backpackers can hike with only a few pounds of gear. Depending on the time of year, the expected weather conditions and how many days I plan to stay on the trail, my pack can range from 15 to 30 pounds.

There are countless ways to reduce pack weight. There are more ways to trim pounds and ounces than trails in the world. And believe it or not, every ounce that could possibly be removed from your back is worth considering, no matter how small. Each backpacker ultimately carries their own weight, and what's right for one person is never what's right for another. It's up to each of us to find out what works best for our own needs and situations.

Outside of pack weight, the planned distance I was to cover was my biggest concern. While I've backpacked longer distances before, I had never done so alone. The FT was not as strenuous as some of the sections commonly found along the Appalachian Trail, but the FT should be taken seriously as backpackers will ascend and descend thousands of feet over the 77 miles through the Appalachian wilderness.

Hiking twice the distance of my last trip, and carrying four more days of food, meant that I would begin the trip with much more weight than I recently become accustomed to carrying. I hoped the lessons learned from my last long-distance trip through the Smoky Mountains a year earlier would carry over to the FT. My goal was to carry less than 30 pounds, which would be difficult considering I needed at least seven days of food to begin the hike.

Many backpackers who attempt the Foothills Trail do so with only a few days of food at a time and rely on drop boxes or hidden caches to resupply. There was no one in the area that I knew to coordinate a resupply with, so I would be forced to carry all seven days of my food at once. As careful as I was in my preparations, I couldn't help but feel that I had again stuffed too much food in my pack.

One of the most notable features of the FT, and perhaps the largest complaint among backpackers, is the hundreds of wooden stairs littered throughout the trail, which has earned it the nickname "The Trail of Stairs."

Natural features, such as the Chattooga River, more than a dozen waterfalls (including upper and lower White Water) and scenic mountaintop views were the true highpoints of the journey, anyway.

I gave myself seven days to complete the trail, which would make it my longest ever solo backpacking trip in terms of both time and distance. Though not the most physically difficult trail in the world, the distance, added weight, isolation and unpredictable spring weather would make this an incredibly difficult challenge.

I chose to hike from Oconee to Table Rock heading west to east for a few reasons. The most important of these was the relative ease of the first 20 or so miles from this direction. The trail here followed along the Chattooga River for many miles, providing a mostly flat riverside experience for the first day and a half. I wanted to make good time to start the hike.

After several weeks of planning and preparation, my dog Raven and I drove off late one Sunday night toward the family farm in upstate South Carolina to stay the night.

***

I arrived at Table Rock State Park in upstate South Carolina to meet my sister Tori who had graciously volunteered to shuttle me from Table Rock to Oconee that morning. For the first time in recent memory, I finally found a shuttle driver whose name was not Mike. I hoped that would not be a bad omen.

After parking and speaking to a ranger about an extended stay in the park, I collected my gear and made one last check of my supplies. The sky overhead was clear, but rain was forecasted for later in the afternoon. A check of the weather on my phone showed a dismal few upcoming days followed by a chilly, but clear, end to the week.

I walked around the nearby ranger station, reading plaques and information boards on the wildlife, natural features and history of the lands that now make up Table Rock.

Table Rock's main attraction was Pinnacle Mountain. At 3,415 feet tall, the mountain is an impressive sight from the park below and one of the tallest mountains in South Carolina. The mountain featured several steep rock walls and even a large cliff called Bald Rock that was visible from the highway. A handful of trails, including the FT, take hikers up and over the mountain. If all went to plan, I would be standing at the overlook on Bald Rock in a week.

The land where Table Rock now sits was once controlled by the

Lower Cherokee around the time of the American Revolution and signs of an even earlier native culture, possibly as old as 3,500 years, were discovered in the park within the last few decades. The Cherokee built no known major settlements here, but the area was home to several hunting camps.

Early southern settlers largely ignored treaties signed by the newly formed American Congress and the native peoples of the lands during the early expansion of the United States, and conflicts continued between the tribes and the southern settlers well into the 1830s when many of the Cherokee and other remaining tribes were forcefully relocated west of the Mississippi after the passage of the Indian Removal Act.

The Trail of Tears and the Indian Removal Act were footnotes in my public education. While those events seemed, at the time at least, so far removed from modern times, those events changed America's course to this day. I couldn't help but wonder what the American Southeast would be like today if the native peoples and the early American settlers had made peace instead of war.

After learning more about the historical significance of the park and the surrounding area, I gained a newfound appreciation for the experience I was about to undertake.

Tori was late. Raven and I meandered through as much of the park as we could close to the parking lot and read through all the information available to us, but more than an hour after our expected meeting time, I still did not see my sister.

A short while later, Tori pulled into the parking lot.

"We went to another parking lot," she told me as she hastily got out of the car. "We waited for more than an hour but you never showed up, so we asked one of the park rangers if there was anywhere else you could be. They sent us this way!"

"It's all right," I told her. I was anxious to start the trail and wanted to set off as soon as possible.

Tori had brought her boyfriend Curtis along for the ride. Both were staying in central North Carolina at the time but were kind enough to accept my offer of $100 for the morning shuttle ride more than a hundred miles away from their home.

Curtis helped me load my bag into the trunk.

Tori and Curtis had both graduated from Clemson University a few months earlier. The pair were starting a new phase in their lives, one of adult responsibilities, bills and building for the future. I'm nine years older than Tori, who is my only full-blooded sibling.

I grabbed a towel for the backseat in case Raven decided to get car sick on the ride and loaded my pack and poles into the trunk. A few moments later, we were off.

Once we were on the road, I caught up with my sister who I had not seen since the previous Christmas. We talked about my upcoming week, video games, job hunting and the family. She and Curtis were trying to figure out the next step in their lives. For both, this meant resumes, applications and interviews.

Curtis had recently flown out west to meet with a tech company and seemed excited by the prospect of packing up and moving across the country to start a new career.

Tori, an artist, was more concerned about the local art and music community than she was with the prospect of finding an entry-level office job somewhere. She seemed willing to go with Curtis wherever his job might take him as long as she could continue to make art and find inspiration in her surroundings.

I had to admit to them that I was jealous of the possibility that they might move to the Pacific Northwest.

An hour or so later, we made it to Oconee. Tori followed the signs toward the Foothills Trail and drove toward the back end of the park where the trailhead was located. Next to the official start of the trail was a large map containing markings highlighting some of the area's better-known attractions.

Tori parked the car, and I walked over to the map. I snapped a quick photo of the board and put my phone in my pocket before heading back to strap on all my gear. I felt a sense of anxious urgency to begin.

After strapping Raven into her pack and gearing up myself, we said our goodbyes and, full of excitement and anticipation, marched off down the hill toward the Chattooga River.

***

The skies overhead had darkened during our ride to Oconee, and a cool spring wind foreshadowed coming rain as we made our way to the river below. The forest around us was beginning the sudden and dramatic awakening from its winter slumber. I could hear birds off in the distance and the occasional squirrel made its way ahead of us on the trail. The leaves on the trees were budding and hints of green were beginning to replace the grey and brown of winter.

The path beneath our feet was clear from fallen leaves and mud. Hiking in spring has its benefits.

The first several miles followed along a gentle downhill slope toward the Chattooga River, the natural border between South Carolina and Georgia. I felt confident as we plodded along, even with my heavy pack and a rambunctious dog bound to my waist.

My goal for the first day was to cover around 16 or so miles to Burrells Ford campground, a large complex of tent sites with picnic tables, a toilet and scenic views of King Creek. Because much of the trail here followed closely beside the Chattooga along the way to Burrells Ford, the elevation profile was not strenuous to begin the day.

The delay at Table Rock that morning meant that I was a little over two hours behind schedule before I had even put boot to ground and, as the skies darkened overhead, the promise of a rain shower threatened to delay me further. I was determined to push on to take advantage of the favorable terrain while we still could, rain or not. Eventually, low, rumbling thunder was heard from off in the distance, filling the valley and trees around me with a grim reminder of nature's potential fury. The signs of coming rain were constant.

After a few hours of relative ease along the trail, the rain finally began to fall. Large drops came from the clouds above which soon gave way to a torrential downpour. Despite protection from my rain jacket and hiker's trucker hat, my clothes and body were soaked after only a few moments.

Poor Raven. She shivered every time we stopped for a brief respite under the trees. We rested frequently to shelter ourselves from the falling rains and continued whenever the skies would relent. Because of this, my pace was dreadful at best. We were on the trail only a few hours, but we were already falling behind the time window we needed to complete the trail.

It felt as though someone was standing above me on a ladder, pouring water out of a never-ending bucket directly onto my head. My rain jacket did its best to keep me dry, but the rain fell with such ferocity that every inch of my body was drenched.

I pushed on as heartily as I could, though Raven had little interest in walking through the continuing downpour and would jump off the trail to find shelter under a bush or tree whenever the opportunity presented itself. Keeping her on track and focused proved difficult. Her feelings directly reflected my own, but she was not aware of how far we still had to go that day.

The rain continued for several hours that afternoon, followed by a lightning storm that began to move overhead in the early evening hours. By the time we made it to the junction with the Chattooga River just after five that afternoon, the thunder and lightning constantly shook and illuminated the river valley around us.

Lightning strikes happened within quick succession, and they were moving closer to us with each strike.

The conditions reminded me of being trapped on top of a ridge in the Appalachian Trail in a lightning storm the spring before. Except for this time, I was not on a heavily trafficked trail with any hope of someone spotting me the next morning if I were to receive an unfortunate shock and keel over. If I were struck and immobilized here, it could be days before someone found me.

I carefully checked my map under my rain jacket and saw that we had made it around 11 miles into the trail by that point in the evening. Continuing in these conditions was not an option.

While the chance of being on the receiving end of a lightning strike when backpacking is minimal, it does happen. I wanted to get as far away from my aluminum trekking poles as possible.

Lightning has claimed only a handful of lives in recent years. Most people who are struck by lightning do survive but often receive neurological and other injuries. Being alone in the woods, without support or even a way to contact someone for help, meant mitigating the risk however possible. That included being, what some might consider, overly cautious during the thunderstorms.

In 2010, hiker Bethany Lott was struck by lightning on North Carolina's Max Patch Bald along the Appalachian Trail during a marriage proposal from her boyfriend Richard Butler. Lott died from the strike moments before Butler planned to present her with an engagement ring. The tragic story received national attention and reminded hikers and backpackers that anyone, anywhere, could be killed by one of Mother Nature's most unpredictable occurrences.

Raven and I passed several riverside spots that would have made for a beautiful camping spot, if not for the rain. We continued the search for a safe spot to set up camp and ride out the storm.

A few dazzling sites were on the bank of the Chattooga and would have made for a lovely campsite on a dry summer's night. The risk of flash flooding, as well as being too close to the water while lightning continued to crack all around us, meant that a more inland and elevated spot would be necessary.

The lightning continued on and off until we came across a large empty site with three or four fire rings and several spots for tents overlooking the river. This discovery coincided with a break in the rain, as well. I decided to take advantage of my good fortune and make camp here.

The rain pattered from the treetops while I searched through my pack to find all of the pieces of gear necessary to set up my tent. The storm eased enough for me to quickly set up what I could without getting the inside of my pack or the inside of my tent too soaked in the process.

Because of the unique shape of my tent, and its lightweight construction, putting it together was more challenging than setting up a traditional two-pole dome tent. Each of the three poles required for assembly was slightly different and had to be inserted into the fabric a particular way. This usually isn't much of a problem, but scrambling in the rain to keep the inside dry made the setup tedious.

Once the tent was put together and its insides protected from the impending rain, I crawled inside with the intention of eating my first real meal of the day.

I pulled out my food bag and ate a Snickers bar and some jerky. My original plan was to cook a dehydrated meal that night, but I was in no mood to sit in the drizzle outside of the tent just for a hot bag of chili mac. I ate nuts, chocolate and junk food instead.

After dinner, Raven and I crawled into the tent, which felt more cramped than usual after bringing my pack inside under the vestibule to protect it from the rain. Paranoid, I placed my hiking poles next to a tree a few dozen yards away from the tent but brought everything else, including my food, inside with me.

Bringing food into a tent, particularly in a place where bears and other animals have complete domain, is never a good idea. But, I thought to myself, if a bear or other wild animal is willing to brave this storm in search of a quick and not-so-easy meal, he deserves one. By this point, I was too cold and wet to care. Besides, Raven would probably scare any animals away.

Raven and I were both miserable. Despite a relatively easy day of hiking in terms of distance and terrain, the cold rain beat us into submission. We spent as much time hiking that day as we had huddled under trees seeking shelter from the rain. The flat trail behind us would have been a breeze in better conditions. I was convinced that we could have made it to Burrells Ford.

I removed most of my clothing and dried off as best I could with a small, microfiber towel. After I was as dry as I could be, I looked through my trail notes and maps. My notes suggested we were still five or so miles away from Burrells Ford campground, well short of the 16 miles that I had planned to achieve that day.

All things considered, I was happy with the distance we covered.

"Maybe we should go back tomorrow," I told Raven as I crawled into my sleeping bag. "I don't think it can get any worse than today. Maybe tomorrow will be better."

The rain continued throughout the night.

***

I awoke the next morning with the rising sun. Thankfully, no water had entered my tent directly, but the condensation that seeped through the tent walls dampened my sleeping bag at the top and bottom of my tent. My clothes, particularly my pants, still felt as though they were fresh from an industrial washing machine. Slipping on a pair of cold, wet pants is not the way anyone wants to start a morning on the trail.

The rain lingered on and off after sunrise. The ground nearby was completely saturated. The morning brought a clearer, albeit dampened view, of the forest around me. We had camped 20 or so yards above the river on a flat section of ground featuring a few tent sites and fire rings. The ground here ran toward the river and sloped down through a clearing toward the water's edge, offering a picturesque view of the river from inside the tent. We were obviously not the first to make use of this spot.

Attempting to sleep through the night's storms had proved difficult as the constant thunder and lightning offered no peace of mind. But despite the poor sleep, my body felt rested and ready for the second day on the trail.

I didn't have the luxury of hiking when I wanted to on this trip. There was a schedule to keep, and further delays meant that I was going to need to make up time somewhere else on the trail. Pushing harder later, during the more difficult sections of trail, was not a pleasant thought, but the previous day had been so miserable that I hoped to carve out some level of enjoyment from the rest of the week. That would start today.

Delaying the start to my second morning would only put me further behind, so I decided to just go, rain or not.

After packing my tent and eating a quick Pop Tart and Clif bar breakfast, Raven and I again set off toward Table Rock around 10 that morning under drizzling grey skies and a cool morning breeze.

The break in the rain was short lived. Just a few steps into the morning's trek, the rain started in full force again, followed by the return of thunder and lightning a half hour later. If any part of me had dried overnight, it was again soaked just moments after beginning the second day on the FT.

We again trudged along for several hours in the rain, occasionally stopping to filter stream water or to hide away under the cover of the above canopy. It was difficult and demoralizing, but we pressed on, hoping for a break in the weather at some point.

I thought back to my recent hike of the Bartram Trail and remembered how difficult it had been to find water along the latter half of the trail. Here, water was everywhere. Small streams collected and flowed alongside the path and fell from the trees above in droves. The Chattooga was nearby and swelled with the runoff from the surrounding hills.

So far, nearly the entire trail had followed closely alongside the Chattooga and streams and other sources of water were plentiful. The fear of being too far from fresh water was officially alleviated. I knew finding water on this trip wouldn't be an issue, but I hadn't thought I would have to deal with constant water instead.

The trail to Burrells Ford campground from my previous night's spot continued to follow alongside the river and was flat and well-maintained. Even with the recent storms, very few trees impeded the trail at any point, and there was the occasional sign of a recently removed fallen tree. I was very impressed with the Foothills Trail Conference and their volunteers for the arduous work they put in toward keeping the trail free of debris and hazards.

I spotted a few river fishermen as we approached the campgrounds who were also braving the rain for the prospect of a few dinner trout. That was a good sign. If there were fishermen in the river, it meant that the campground or a parking lot was close. I waved as we passed by from the forest above, but decided against stopping to bother the fishermen.

In the early afternoon, we finally arrived at Burrells Ford, a sprawling campground situated against the Chattooga River that featured a variety of large tenting sites. The skies had cleared during the early afternoon and the rains seemed to be taking a break, as well.

My spirits lifted as for the first time in nearly two days. We had a break in the weather, and I wanted to take advantage of the facilities while at the campground.

I debated on whether to stay the night at Burrells Ford. If I were to complete the trail on time, I would need to push on for another six miles or more before the end of the second day. I had no idea if the rains were going to continue or worsen before I made it that far. My instincts told me to stop, but there was a burning desire to finish what I started.

I removed my pack, smoked a cigarette and paced around the parking lot for a while, before fully accepting the decision to cut the trip short and stay here for at least the night. I was crushed but relieved to know that I wouldn't have to push myself to exhaustion or night hike in the rain to make up any lost ground. Competing with the weather was a fool's errand, and I wanted no more part of it.

Raven and I surveyed the cars parked in the gravel lot as we made our way to the campground gate. A few men in their late 40s were unloading a truck with camping supplies and placing them in a rugged outdoor wagon to take back down the hill to the campsites.

"Hey, buddy," one of the men called over to me as I paced around the grounds' information board. "Are you hiking the trail?"

"I was," I told him. "I think I'm going to cut my trip short and camp here for a day or two and try to find a ride back up to the road. The weather has been brutal. I came from Oconee yesterday, and it's rained the entire time."

The two men introduced themselves as John and Rich.

"You look like you could use a beer," John told me. He reached into a cooler from his trunk and handed me a Coors Light, which

I happily accepted. John became my new best friend.

We talked about the trail conditions behind me, the weather, his family's plans and Burrells Ford.

Rich was a heavier fellow than John, hiding a slightly balding head under a Braves baseball cap. He was wearing shorts and a t-shirt and looked as though he had been in the woods for a few days already. John was thinner, taller and wore some sort of adventuring shirt and cargo shorts like you might find at an outfitters shop next to a mall. He wasn't out of place in the forest, but he and Rich seemed an odd couple based on appearance alone.

John and Rich told me they had come to this site as children, both members of the same Boy Scout troop and became lifelong friends who carried their love of camping and nature into adulthood.

Now, the pair still came up once a year in the spring, bringing their families along for a week of outdoor exploring, camping and a break from their hectic lives back home.

"We mostly just relax," Rich told me. "We fish, hike and do whatever. The point of being up here is to just be here."

"I completely understand that," I responded.

After explaining the difficulty of the past two days, John made another offer I couldn't refuse.

"You should just stay here. It's going to rain all night again, and we're making sausage for dinner. At least you can go to bed full."
I happily agreed.

I walked with John and Rich down the gravel road toward the campsites while Raven followed behind. Convinced that she would not run away, I removed her leash for the walk down.

The path here was an old forest service road that was gated off from the parking lot back up the hill. A quarter mile or so from the parking lot, down a steep hill, a series of large campsites appeared off to our left and right.

John's site was the first to appear. It was massive. He and his family had set up near a small creek running through the campground close to the entrance. He had brought two large tents, each capable of holding four or more people comfortably, set up underneath the largest tarp I've ever seen. Toward the back of the tent pad was a hammock beside a fire ring and picnic table.

"How long did it take you to get the tarp up?"

"A few hours," John replied. "I learned a couple of years ago that if we were going to be out here for a whole week, we needed a tarp."

"It took him a couple of years to get it right," his wife added as we arrived. "But he's got a pretty good system now. We've never had a problem with it falling or collecting any water. That's why we bring the ladder."

Sure enough, an old wooden ladder was propped against a tree just off the tent pad.

Rich, on the other hand, needed far fewer luxuries. His tent pad was one site over and only featured a dome tent and a few supplies scattered on a picnic table nearby. He had a larger cooler and not much else. Rich and his son were the only occupants of this site. "Why don't you go set up your stuff and come back for food?" John suggested. "We'll start on dinner and hopefully be done by the time you're done."

I smiled and headed off to find my own corner of the campground.

I followed the gravel path toward the river past a handful of occupied sites and set up as close to the water as I could find. If I was going to sacrifice time on the trail for the comfort of a well-equipped campsite, I could at least find a spot with the best possible view.

A few of the sites were littered with garbage and other bits of trash. Most of this had been relegated to the fire pits, but a few bits of rubbish were scattered along the campsite path, as well. Despite being far off in the woods, well removed from even the closest forest service road, the campground carried the different feeling of being not-quite-remote thanks to the occupants and leftover bits of rubbish.

I set up my tent with the door facing the stream and secured the tent to the ground. A few hours had passed since any rain fell from overhead, but I sensed more was on the way. I quickly set up my rainfly, removed what I needed from my pack and hung my food on a nearby bear pole a dozen or so yards away from the tent.

Before heading back to meet up with John and his family, I collected as much burnable firewood as I could carry. Campsites like these are typically picked clean of anything substantial to burn in colder months, but the winds and storms from the last few days had knocked plenty of smaller sticks and twigs from the trees high above. Most of what I collected was wet but would dry quickly under a tarp or if kept beside a fire.

Raven and I walked back to John's site where his son, a tall, lanky 12 or 13-year-old, was manning a propane grill. He was cooking sausage, sautéing onions and toasting hot dog buns.

After nearly two full days in the woods, most of that hiking through backcountry, the extras here felt a bit like cheating. I was thankful to have something other than granola bars, jerky, chocolate and nuts to eat for dinner.

We sat around the fire chatting about family, backpacking, the trials and tribulations of becoming an Eagle Scout and camp food until dusk slowly transitioned into the night. Raven and I made our way back to the tent in the dark, my belly full, after saying our goodbyes and thanking John and his family for their hospitality and company that evening.

Back at my own campsite, I filtered two liters of water from the stream. I sat in my tent for a while under the glow of my headlamp, inspecting my maps and calculating how far each remaining day would need to be if I were to finish on time. I was still several miles behind, and the next day's hike would be an intense uphill section away from the Chattooga toward the North Carolina border.

I resigned myself to staying at the campgrounds for another day to explore my immediate surroundings instead of pushing to the next campsite. I would hike back toward the road the following day if I couldn't find a ride from a fisherman or hiker.

The rain returned not long after the darkness overtook the forest. The occasional drop of water somehow found its way through my tarp and onto my head or sleeping bag. Despite the wet weather, sleeping that night proved far easier than my first night on the trail.

***

It rained throughout the night. My tent, as light and as compact as can be, did not do a decent job of keeping water out during my second night in the forest. A constant drip seeped through the top of tent wall despite my tarp's best efforts to keep me dry. Perhaps my tent was tired and gave in to the rains, as well.

Raven stirred to begin the morning. After the last two early days followed by several miles of hiking, she picked up on the routine but was not at all interested in tackling a third day in the forest. She was slow and sluggish, not at all her usual self.

All motivation for leaving the comfort of my sleeping bag was sapped, as well. Checking my phone, I saw that it was just after seven in the morning. Despite the overnight rain, the storm seemed to have moved away from us by daybreak, at least for the time being, but I was keen to stay inside the tent and sleep for as long as possible.

I drifted in and out for the next hour or so until I heard approaching footsteps.

"Good morning," a voice called out as a man approached my tent. "Morning," I sleepily replied as I unzipped the front door to poke my head out. It was John, standing above me holding a carafe.

"Would you like some coffee? We made too much, and I thought you might want some."

The pot steamed from the spout as John held it in front of him. I was taken aback once again by John's show of hospitality. He either felt bad for me or thought I was out of my element at the campsite.

Either way, I graciously accepted the offer and sipped away from my cooking pot.

"Any problems with the rain?" he asked after I had dressed and climbed out of the tent.

"My tent leaked. I've got a pretty big puddle in there," I said, pointing inside.

"Oh, that's too bad," he responded. "What do you have for breakfast?"

"Oh, I have some Pop Tarts, I think. Maybe a Clif bar. I'm not sure yet."

"Well, if you want something hot, we're making bacon, eggs and toast," he offered.

I thanked him for the breakfast invitation but told him I wasn't particularly hungry just yet. In truth, I felt bad that he and his family were so generous. An early-morning coffee would go a long way in subsiding any hunger, and since we weren't hitting the trail to start the day, I didn't feel the need to eat so soon after waking.

After finishing the coffee and drying what I could from the inside of my tent, Raven and I set off to explore the area around the campsite.

With nowhere in particular to go, and no set schedule to adhere to, I walked around the campground to check out the other campers nearby. Most of the sites were occupied, but nearly everyone in the grounds had yet to start their mornings.

We passed beside a trail marker pointing off in the direction of King Creek Falls only a few yards away from where we camped the night before. I decided to follow the sign and set off up the trail.

The path followed along King Creek for a mile or so east and away from the Chattooga River. The trail was easy to navigate and relatively level. After walking for 30 minutes or so, the waterfall came into view through the trees ahead. Though only 70 feet tall, the tiered rocks provided a spectacular show from the creek below.

If there was one good thing about the non-stop rain of the last few days, it was the swelled creek waters and the full flow of the waterfall now high above us. In the summer or early fall, the water here would not be nearly as intense or the experience quite as spectacular.

I had brought along a few snacks and a bottle of water for the short hike, leaving my heavy pack and most of its contents inside of my tent. After securing Raven to a nearby tree, I sat down next to her and gazed at the waterfall above for nearly an hour, relaxing in the warm, mid-morning sun.

It felt good to be out of the rain for a while.

Eventually, we headed back to the campground to spend the rest of the afternoon.

After returning from King Creek, the rain returned. I crawled inside my tent and napped for a few hours before lunch to wait out the drizzle.

***

When I woke up, I decided to make my way to the local trout fish hatchery four or so miles up the Foothills Trail to see if I could use their phone to call a shuttle driver to pick me up and take me back to Table Rock. My phone had not had a signal since before I arrived at Table Rock several days earlier, and the hatchery was the only place I could think of nearby that would have a phone.

After packing up my gear, I walked over to John and his family, who were getting ready to set off on their own afternoon hike, to again thank them for their hospitality and say goodbye. John and his wife wished us luck as we marched up the hill back to the trail.

My pack and its contents were mostly dry by this point in the afternoon, which meant my load was several pounds lighter now than it had been during the last two rain-soaked days. I was even able to hike without my rain jacket for the first time during the entire trip.

Raven and I were back on the Foothills Trail after a leisurely day napping, snacking and waterfall gazing. The FT in the section following Burrells Ford was strenuous and climbed upward nearly the entire trek out from the campground. We stopped frequently to breathe and to rest our legs as we continued upward and onward. The afternoon sun cut through the clouds above, leaving only blue skies and dissipating clouds. For the first time since leaving Oconee State Park, the weather was pleasant.

Water became scarce as we moved further from the river below, despite the recent rains. Thankfully, I had filtered some two liters at the campground earlier in the day, but the muggy, warm afternoon required several water breaks. One benefit from the past few days was the plentiful water along the trail. Moving away from the river also meant moving away from readily available water.

The junction to the fish hatchery road was just over three miles from Burrells Ford, but the hike seemed to go on for an eternity. The nonstop uphill climb reminded me of the Appalachian Trail through the Smoky Mountains or hiking up Slaughter Mountain during our Coosa Backcountry Trail hike earlier in the year.

We had left the campground just after noon, and by two in the afternoon, I guessed that we were still more than a mile away from the junction to the fish hatchery. The trail was rough and rocky, covered in roots and loose stone.

Just before three that afternoon, after a few too many breaks, we finally arrived at the top of the hill and came to the paved road that intersected with the fish hatchery. From what I had learned from John earlier in the day, the hatchery closed to the public at four, so I marched down the hill toward the facility as quickly as my legs would allow.

The road curved into the valley below, sharply cutting left and right as it made its way back toward the river from the ridgeline. A short while later, we arrived at the hatchery gate and walked into the sprawling concrete complex. There were several buildings surrounding many large water-filled trout fish pens. Each pen held trout of varying sizes. Some of the pens housed fish larger than any you might see in the Chattooga or other Appalachian rivers while others contained smaller and smaller fish until they reached the size of minnows.

I brought Lucy here more than a year earlier during one of our weekend outings in the area and spent a fair amount of time inspecting each pen while Lucy threw handfuls of food pellets into the water. The fish, ever-anxious for a meal, would jostle and hurl themselves out of the water itself while attempting to snap up one of the pellets.

Toward the far end of the pens was an administrative office with a U.S. Forest Service truck parked in front. I walked to the office, removed my pack, secured Raven to a bench outside and knocked on the door. Inside, a couple of hatchery workers were standing around discussing the business of the day.

"Hey there," I said to one of the hatchery workers as I entered the building. "I'm backpacking the Foothills Trail, and I don't think I'll be able to make it back to my car on schedule. I was hoping that I could use your phone to call a shuttle driver."

The hatchery employee happily obliged.

The Foothills Trail guidebook I purchased before my trip featured a few numbers of volunteers and shuttle drivers. I first called

Heyward Douglass, the Executive Director of the Foothills Trail Conference, to see if he could help me find a shuttle back to my car at Table Rock. Dave was a well-known outdoorsman in the area and the person I knew would be the most helpful.

He answered the phone from the top of South Carolina's tallest point, a windy Sassafras Mountain.

"Hello?" Dave answered.

"Mr. Heyward," I began. "My name is Ryan Watkins, and I'm on the Foothills Trail at the Walhalla State Fish Hatchery. I'm trying to find a shuttle from here to Table Rock. Do you think you could help me out?"

"Well, I'm up on Sassafras at the commissioning right now. When do you need a shuttle?" I later learned that Dave and other trail volunteers were commissioning a large overlook on the top of Sassafras.

"I was hoping for today, but I can do tomorrow if that's not possible."

"Hold on, let me see what I can do." And with that, Dave hung up.

I sat in the hatchery office for a few moments in silence before the phone rang again.

"So, I reached out to the group, and Mike can come get you this evening," Dave told me.

"Mike?"

"Yeah, he's one of the volunteers who runs a shuttle service for hikers." Dave read out Mike's number to me. I couldn't believe that I would have another driver named Mike.

"Thanks, Dave. I really appreciate this," I told him before hanging up the phone.

I called Mike and arranged to meet him back up the hill by the FT junction I had come out an hour or so earlier. I quickly thanked the men in the hatchery, strapped on my pack and headed back up the hill to the junction.

We arrived at the trail junction an hour or so before Mike was scheduled to meet me. The hike out from the hatchery along the paved road was backbreaking. We had pushed hard that afternoon to make it to the hatchery before it closed, and now we were climbing back up the mountain to meet Mike.

Raven and I sat down to rest and wait for the shuttle.

Mike arrived less than an hour later. He was older, tall and grey. He carried decades of hiking and backpacking experience with him and exuded the confidence of a well-worn man. A former Appalachian Trail thru hiker, Mike spent much of his time these days hiking and volunteering with the Foothills Trail Conference, helping maintain the trail whenever possible.

He drove a white Dodge minivan and made a point to caution me that it had been recently cleaned while I loaded my pack into the back of the van. He joked that his wife would be upset if the carpets were sullied when he returned home that evening.

I kicked the mud off my boots as best I could and wiped Raven down with a towel before we hopped in the van to head back to Table Rock.

The ride began in silence. I was physically exhausted and hesitated to initiate a conversation. It felt nice to sit on a soft chair for a while.

Finally, Mike spoke. "So, why'd you cut your trip early?"

For his part, Mike was understanding about my decision to end the hike at the hatchery and return home. He was less sympathetic about my fear of being struck by lightning.

"You know, the chances of getting struck by lightning are almost nothing," he told me.

"Oh, I know," I responded. "But, I didn't feel safe. If I was with a group, we probably would have kept going. It's tough when you're out there by yourself for days in the rain."

He told me about his time on the Appalachian Trail and how he had been stranded on top of a North Carolina bald during a fierce early-spring thunderstorm. Of all his experiences, that, Mike said, was his most terrifying moment in the backcountry.

I told him about my recent backpacking trip along the Bartram Trail and my Appalachian Trail section hike through the Smoky Mountains a year earlier where I was also caught on a mountaintop thunderstorm.

He had many stories to share. We discussed his favorite sections of the AT and the Foothills Trail, his current work as a shuttle driver and his involvement with the organization that maintains and cares for the FT.

It was hard not to be envious of him. His story was interesting. Mike lived an adventurous life in retirement and found an opportunity to be in nature, both as a hobby and a way to earn a little money, long after moving on from his professional career.

I thought about my future life and what retirement might look like for me. Would I own and operate a hostel? Maybe become a shuttle driver for backpackers along the AT?

An hour or so after we set off from the fish hatchery, we pulled into the Table Rock parking lot. Mike knew the park ranger on duty and went to talk to him while I loaded my pack, poles and Raven into the Jeep.

The last three days were exhaustive. Though we only hiked 22 or so miles of the planned 77, my legs and shoulders felt as though I had just come off a month-long stint of backpacking.

The constant rains during our time on the trail soaked me to the core.

It felt like Raven and I spent as much time standing under the cover of trees as moving forward over the last few days. My recent hike of the Bartram Trail, though much longer in distance, did not have the same effect on my body.

Despite sitting in a dry, warm van for the last hour, my clothes were still damp.

I was looking forward to a hot shower, a warm meal and a soft place to sleep that night.

The trip was not a complete failure, but it certainly felt like one after saying goodbye to Mike and beginning the drive back to Atlanta. I drove home in silence while Raven slept in the passenger's seat.

Our journey home took only a few hours, but the rains continued throughout the drive and well into the remainder of the week. I took comfort in knowing that even if we stayed on the trail and pushed as hard as we could, it would have been a miserable experience. A small part of me wanted to turn the car around and try again.

After making it home and reflecting on the journey, I vowed to someday return to the Foothills Trail to complete what I started, this time with a little more consideration for the weather.

***

It would be several months before I would again tackle another hiking trail. The lingering memories of my disappointment on the Foothills Trail and the coming sweltering summer months provided an ever-ready excuse to spend time doing other, less fulfilling things.

Life returned to its boring normal. I settled into my nine to five routine, dance lessons and Girl Scout meetings on the weekends, work and responsibility during the week. I played video games, spent time with friends and occasionally wrote.

But as the cooler months returned, the forest and mountains once again called. It became impossible to ignore. I would put my failures behind me and again seek adventure.

It began slowly at first, an afternoon hike through the nearby Vickery Creek trail network in North Atlanta with Lucy or a quick spell at Brasstown Falls while visiting the family farm. Eventually, I found myself spending more and more time in the forest on the weekends.

Many months after returning home empty-handed and disappointed from my Foothills Trail experience, I again set off to discover more tales from southern trails.

About the Author

Ryan Watkins was born in Athens, Georgia and is a former journalist for a variety of print and web publications. An avid outdoorsman, Ryan spends much of his free time hiking, exploring, writing and photographing the Southeast's most famous waterfalls.

Ryan is also the author of "The Longest Mile: Nine Days in the Great Smoky Mountains."

More information available at mryanwatkins.com.

Made in the USA
Columbia, SC
30 December 2017